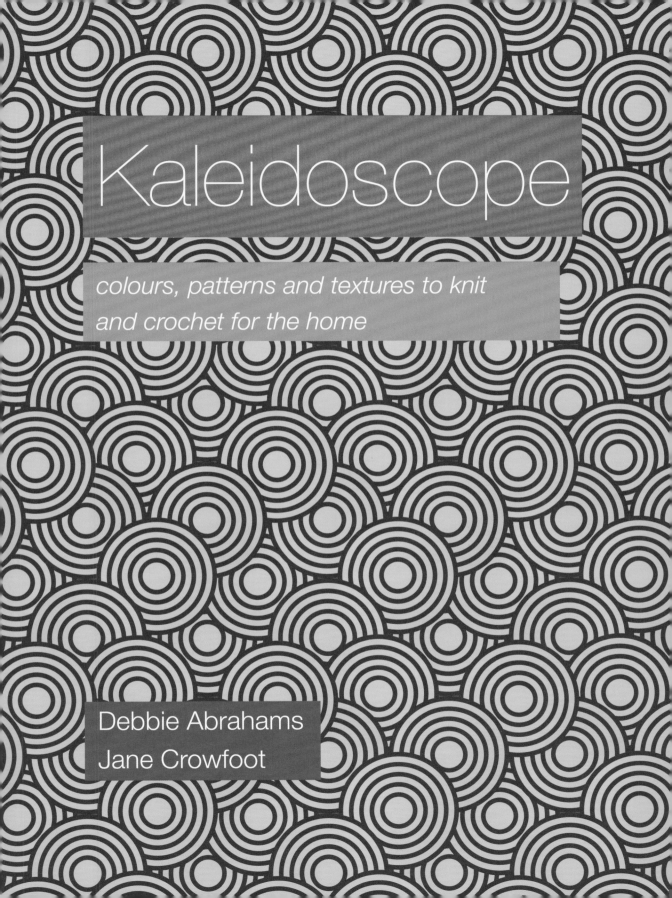

Kaleidoscope

colours, patterns and textures to knit and crochet for the home

Debbie Abrahams

Jane Crowfoot

Foreword

As Brand Manager for Rowan Yarns I am very proud to have been asked to write the foreword for this beautiful book, Kaleidoscope, which completely lives up to its name; page after page Debbie and Jane inspire with their bright and contemporary collection of home accessories.

I feel personally connected to both of these talented designers since I was lucky enough to hire them as Rowan Design Consultants back in the mid 1990s when the Rowan Consultancy was in its infancy. Debbie and Jane proved invaluable assets to the team, teaching, demonstrating and guiding consumers in all their knitting and crochet adventures.

Their respective careers have gone from strength to strength with Debbie and Jane offering a wide range of events, workshops and design back catalogues. They have both written best selling books within the world of knitting and crochet and offer people all over the world access to their exclusive clubs; Debbie runs a thriving Mystery Blanket Club for knitters, taking them on a journey to complete an exclusive design over 10 months, whilst Jane runs an equally popular Crochet Club which presents crocheters with a special project over the course of 6 months.

Jane & Debbie are close friends, they work really well together and – as you will see from the designs within this book – their design styles are an absolute compliment to each other. This is their first joint book and they have succeeded in bringing their own unique design talent across both crochet and knitting skills. Rowan are proud to have been able to support them through such a wonderful project.

I hope that everybody will enjoy Kaleidoscope as much as my team at Rowan and I have.

Regards

Kate Buller
Brand Manager
Rowan Yarns

KALEIDOSCOPE
colours, patterns and textures to knit
and crochet for the home

This edition published in 2013 by
Inspired Minds Publishing
51 Bevan Road
Cockfosters
Hertfordshire
EN4 9DY

Produced in association with Quail Publishing
www.QuailBooks.com

Designer	Darren Brant
Editor	Juliet Bernard
Photography	Michael Wicks
Styling	Debbie Abrahams & Jane Crowfoot
Pattern Editor	Luise Roberts
Charts	Luise Roberts
Location	ClearSpace - The Tea House
Illustration	Saskia van Cleef-Megens, Orname & JNK Artworks

British Library Cataloguing in Publication Data
A catalogue record of this book is available from the
British Library

ISBN 978-0-9571659-0-8

Reproduced and printed in the United Kingdom by
Butler Tanner & Dennis - Frome, England

CONTENTS

Introduction

Welcome to our world

Friends for many years, we first met when we both worked as Design Consultants for Rowan Yarns. We soon realized that we not only shared common interests outside of work, but also had very similar ideas in terms of our own individual design aspirations. Debbie launched her Mystery Blanket Club in 2008, which was an instant global success, followed by Jane's equally successful Crochet Club in 2011. Both clubs have worldwide appeal and have generated interest in contemporary knit and crochet projects for the home. It goes without saying that we share an intuitive passion for craft, which has now led to an inevitable partnership culminating in our first book title together, Kaleidoscope.

Following a visit to Poitiers in France we decided to use a shared inspiration as the basis for Kaleidoscope. We agreed on a set of inspirational images to design projects using a shared colour palette and developed our ideas in knit and crochet. We envisaged a ground breaking collection of projects that would push the boundaries of what is already available in the world of knit and crochet.

With current trends in mind we have created designs that we feel will not only encourage knitters and crocheters to try new techniques, but will give them hours of pleasure producing sophisticated, contemporary accessories for their homes. This collection has given us both the opportunity to design in a way that has ensured each and every project is one that we are immensely proud of.

We see this book as the foundation of an exciting future and it is our hope that it will form the basis of a new and fulfilling venture together. We hope that knitters and crocheters everywhere will join us on our thrilling journey.

Debbie & Jane

Lolly ~ pg. 108

Debbie: vibrant stocking stitch stripes in a soft wool yarn result in an eye-catching bag that is easy to knit. It is large enough to carry all your essentials on a day out and will certainly get people asking "Where did you buy that bag?"

Wiggle ~ pg. 88

Jane: warm rich shades of yarn worked in a chevron stitch combine to make this simple yet striking sofa cushion cover. Great for using up odds and ends from your stash, and it's easy to do a colour swap to create some wonderful variations.

Quiver ~ pg. 118

Debbie: this vibrantly coloured table runner is a great way to spice up your dining-room table, adding a touch of flair to meal-times, whatever the occasion.

Skittle ~ pg. 64

Jane: I believe that you can never have too much of a good thing and that there is definitely no such thing as too many beads! This table runner uses two of my favorite beads shades from Debbie's wonderful collection.

Yo Yo ~ pg. 110

Debbie: I love playing with counter-colour changes as the effects can be so amazing. For this floor cushion I chose to work with just two colour palettes – pinks and greys – and had great fun swapping them around to create a design that is balanced and harmonious in both its geometric shapes and colours.

Giggle ~ pg. 86

Jane: smooth over the duvet and slip one of these onto your pillow in the morning and your bed will be instantly 'made' with no need for fancy cushions or throws. Make them in lots of colour ways and fold them by the bed at night.

Zap ~ pg. 92

Debbie: for me there are no rules when it comes to mixing different fibres together in one project – it simply makes it more fun, and the possibilities are endless! So I really enjoyed designing this bed runner and did just that, combining smooth cottons with soft wool yarns.

Poppet ~ pg. 62

Jane: a perfect size for use as a handbag and large enough to squeeze in your crochet hooks, knitting needles and a few balls of yarn, this bag is a quick and easy project which also acts as a great introduction to crochet colour work.

Groovy ~ pg. 104

Debbie: this cushion is really fun to knit and would make the perfect accessory for a boy or girl's bedroom. The intriguing thing about this design is how all the segments work together to create the circular panels – genius and crazy at the same time!

Hoopla ~ pg. 75

Jane: I love the way the tweedy yarn sits alongside the single colour yarn to create the triangular shapes within this bolster. Squares are made separately then sewn together so its deceptively easy too!

Flash ~ pg. 113

Debbie: this case can be used to keep a variety of things clean and cosy including tablets, diaries and notebooks. Quick and easy to knit, it is a great way for the novice knitter to get to grips with stripes and textured stitches in the round.

Pippin ~ pg. 60

Jane: a really simple project, great to make in front of
the TV or when your concentration level is a little low –
honestly you really can't go too far wrong! Try mixing lots
of colours to get fantastic stripe sequences.

Mallow ~ pg. 114

Debbie: this design was inspired by a painted pillar in a church that Jane and I visited during a trip to France. It really caught my eye, not only because of the simplicity of the shapes, but also because of the optical illusion created by the clever use of colour. I used the same balance of colours in my design to achieve this effect.

Wheezer ~ pg. 70

Jane: bright pixie green and cream combine with a hint of
citrus orange to create this mammoth floor cushion ideal
for brightening up a room and adding a touch of zig zag
fun! Great for kids who can't sit still on the sofa!

Zing ~ pg. 98

Debbie: pink and grey stripes are brought to life with flashes of lime green in a strict stripe pattern using crisp cotton yarns. The stripes are studded with pink and white beads to add extra colour and texture to the bolster.

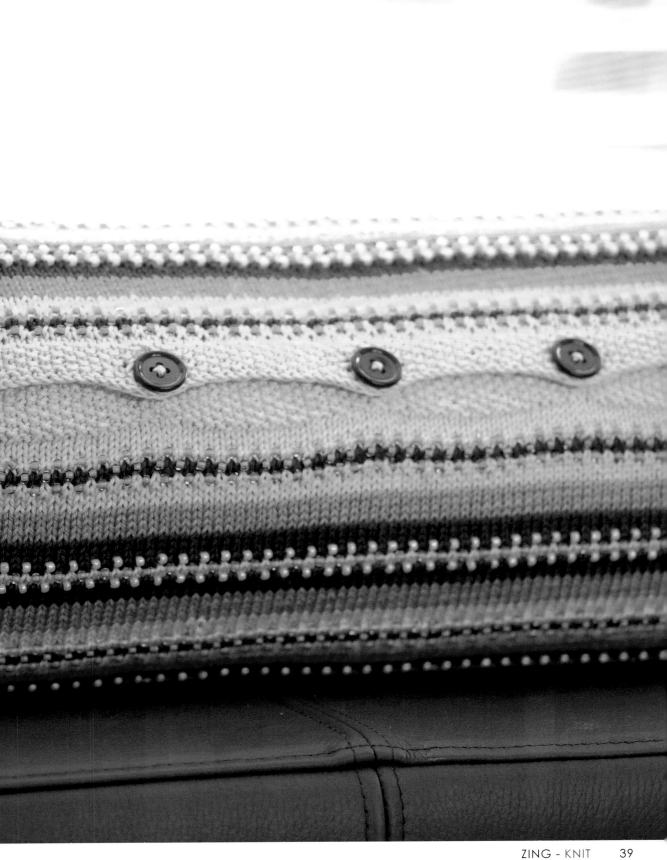

Kicker ~ pg. 72

Jane: this snug blanket is perfect for those chilly winter evenings – the colours and soft yarn will perk up your mood, keep you warm, and brighten even the darkest and coldest of dismal days!

Pizzazz ~ pg. 116

Debbie: knitting is always so much more interesting when an assortment of different stitches are combined together in one design, which is why I found the pillow slip so enjoyable to knit. The starting point is a pretty beaded cast-on followed by a zig-zag chevron pattern, beaded stripes and miniature beaded cables – never a dull moment!

Giddy ~ pg. 80

Jane: I wanted to create an optical illusion within this easy crochet project – sometimes you can see a lattice, other times you can see blocks in a brick pattern. I really enjoyed designing this blanket!

Spangle ~ pg. 94

Debbie: for me the thrill of working with geometric shapes is seeing what happens when they are placed next to each other, creating a tessellation. This blanket is made up of two blocks that when joined together create a series of perfect triangles in an all-over colourful design.

Bebop ~ pg. 78

Jane: the effectiveness of this beaded fan pattern came as a delightful surprise. The addition of beads to this relatively simple design makes the notebook cover exciting and fun to make.

Dazzle ~ pg. 120

Debbie: brighten up your living room with this beaded and textured zig-zag cushion cover. You can choose to knit it in the colours as shown or use your own combination. It's a great way to try multi-colour beading if you have never tried this technique before.

Waffle ~ pg. 68

Jane: I just love putting pink and green together! Add a bit of dark blue and a bright green into the mix and all the colours will sing out in unison, in a wonderful collaboration. It seems a shame to just sit on it!

Nifty ~ pg. 100

Debbie: large interlocking crosses create a bold design using a minimal colour palette of blues, green and cream. It is handy for use both indoors and out - so comfortable!

Crackle ~ pg. 82

Jane: as soon as I saw the inspiration for this cushion
I knew exactly what I wanted the project to look like.
Imagine how wonderfull various colour combinations
would be together on a sofa.

CROCHET
PATTERNS

PIPPIN RUNNER pg. 32

Jane: even though it's fairly long, this bed runner grows pretty quickly because of the use of treble crochet (US double crochet). Lots of crocheters struggle to keep the side edges straight – remember to miss the stitch at the base of the turning chain at the beginning of the row and to make the final stitch of the row into the turning chain made on the row before – if in doubt count!

Measurements
Finished size approximately 36 x 200cm
(14⅛ x 78¾in)

Materials
Yarn
Rowan Cotton Glace: 50g (1¾oz) ball(s)

A	Ecru 725 (cream)	10
B	Blood Orange 445 (deep red)	3
C	Persimmon 832 (orange)	3
D	Black 727 (black)	1

Equipment
3mm (US C-2) crochet hook
2.5mm (US 1/0) crochet hook
Knitter's sewing or tapestry needle

Tension
22 sts and 24 rows to 10cm (4in) square
over double crochet using 3mm (US C-2)
crochet hook.

Special abbreviation
mb = make bobble: work 5 incomplete treble
crochet stitches into the next st so that 6 loops
remain on the hook, yarn around hook and draw
through all the loops on the hook.

Method
Using 3mm (US C-2) hook and yarn A, make 77ch.
Row 1 (RS): skip 1ch, 1dc into each ch to end of row, turn. (76 sts)
Row 2: 3ch (counts as 1tr), skip st at base of beg-3ch, 1tr into each st to end, turn.
Row 3: 1ch (do not count as st), 1dc into each st to end, turn.
Rows 4–5: repeat the last 2 rows once more, changing to yarn B on the last st, turn.
Work rows 6–19 as row 3, 1dc into each st in the following colour sequence:
Row 6–7: yarn B, changing to yarn C on the last st, turn.
Row 8: yarn C, changing to yarn A on the last st, turn.
Row 9–10: yarn A, changing to yarn C on the last st, turn.
Row 11: yarn C, changing to yarn B on the last st, turn.
Row 12–13: yarn B, changing to yarn C on the last st, turn.
Row 14: yarn C, changing to yarn A on the last st, turn.
Row 15–16: yarn A, changing to yarn C on the last st, turn.
Row 17: yarn C, changing to yarn B on the last st, turn.
Row 18–19: yarn B, changing to yarn A on the last st, turn.
Continue as follows:
Row 20: yarn A, 1ch (do not count as st), 1dc into each st to end, turn.
Row 21: 3ch (counts as 1tr), skip st at base of beg-3ch, 1tr into each st to end, turn.
Rows 22–23: repeat the last 2 rows.
Row 24 (WS): 1ch (do not count as st), *1dc into each next 10 sts, using short length of yarn D, mb into next st; repeat from * 5 times more, 1dc into each next 10 sts, turn.
Row 25: yarn A, repeat row 21.
Row 26: 1ch (do not count as st), 1dc into each st to end, turn.
Rows 27–28: repeat the last 2 rows.
Rows 29–46: repeat rows 6–23.
Row 47 (RS): yarn A, 1ch (do not count as st), *1dc into each next 10 sts, using short length of yarn D, mb into next st; repeat from * 5 times more, 1dc into each next 10 sts, turn.
Rows 48–51: repeat rows 25–28.
Repeat rows 6–51, 7 times more.
Repeat rows 6–24, omitting bobbles on the final repeat of row 24 and replacing them with dc sts.
Fasten off.

Making up
Weave in yarn ends.
Block and press using the preferred method, taking care not to flatten the bobbles with excess pressure.

Edging

With RS facing, using 2.5mm (US 1/0) hook and yarn A, join in yarn.

Round 1: work evenly spaced dc around outside edge with 3dc into each corner, changing to yarn C on the last st, ss into top of first dc to join.

Round 2: 1ch (do not count as st) 1dc into each st and 3dc into each corner st, to end, changing to yarn B on the last st, ss into top of first dc to join.

Rounds 3–4: 1ch (do not count as st) 1dc into each st and 3dc into each corner st, to end, ss into top of first dc to join. Fasten off.

POPPET BAG pg. 24

Jane: this small bag is worked in the round and so does not have any seams to sew up once you've finished with your hook! It makes a good introduction to crochet colour work, but be sure to use markers all the time to indicate where the row change over is made – it's a bit easy to get carried away, so be careful!

Measurements

Finished size approximately 32 x 22.5cm (12½ x 9in)

Materials

Yarn

Rowan Creative Focus Worsted:
100g (3½oz) ball(s)

A	Golden Heather 00018 (old gold)	1
B	Saffron 03810 (yellow)	1
C	Magenta 01890 (dark pink)	1
D	New Fern 01265 (green)	1
E	Cobalt 01107 (dark turquoise)	1

Other

Fabric for lining, 100% cotton, ½m (½yd) of 112cm (44in) wide fabric
Iron on interfacing for medium-weight fabric, 5 x 64cm (2 x 25in)
Bag handles, sew on black leather, 71cm (28in)
Magnetic bag clasp, sew on with leather surround, 14mm (⅝in)

Equipment

4mm (US G-6) crochet hook
Stitch markers, two
Knitter's sewing or tapestry needle
Sewing needle and matching thread

Tension

19 sts and 20 rows to 10cm (4in) square over double crochet using 4mm (US G-6) crochet hook.

Note

This project is worked in the round using double crochet and a slip stitch into the first dc to join the round. Do not to work into the starting chain at the end of the round.

Method

Using yarn A, make 46ch.

Foundation round: skip 1ch, work 1dc into each next 44ch, 3dc into next ch, do not turn, work double crochet along remaining side of each foundation ch, working 3dc into the final ch, ss to first dc to join. (94 sts) Place stitch marker into the centre st of both groups of 3dc. Remove the markers before working the marked sts and replace into the centre st after working the marked sts.

Round 1: 1ch (do not count as st), 1dc into st at base of beg-1ch, *1dc into each st to next marker, 3dc into marked st; repeat from *, 1dc into each st to end of round, ss into top of first dc to join. (98 sts) Repeat the last round 6 times more. (122 sts)

Rounds 8–23: 1ch (do not count as st), 1dc into st at base of beg-1ch, 1dc into each st to end of round, ss into top of first dc to join. After working marked stitches in next round, stitch markers are no longer required.

Round 24: 1ch (do not count as st), 1dc into st at base of beg-1ch, 1dc into each next 49 sts, dc2tog over next 2 sts, 1dc into each next 59 sts, dc2tog over next 2 sts, 1dc into next 9 sts, ss into top of first dc to join. (120 sts)

Work the following rounds using the intarsia method, yarns A and B, and changing yarn colour on the last st before the colour change.

Round 25 (colour pattern set): yarn A, 1ch (do not count as st), 1dc into st at base of beg-1ch, 1dc into each next 3 sts, *yarn B, 1dc into next st, yarn A, 1dc into each next 7 sts; repeat from * 13 times more, yarn B, 1dc into next st, yarn A, 1dc into next 3 sts, ss into top of first dc to join.

Round 26: yarn A, 1ch (do not count as st), 1dc into st at base of beg-1ch, 1dc into each next 3 sts, *yarn B, 1dc into each next 2 sts, yarn A, 1dc in each next 6 sts; repeat from * 13 times more, yarn B, 1dc in each next 2 sts, yarn A, 1dc in next 2 sts, ss into top of first dc to join.

Round 27: yarn A, 1ch (do not count as st), 1dc into st at base of beg-1ch, 1dc into each next 3 sts, *yarn B, 1dc in each next 3 sts, yarn A, 1dc in each next 5 sts; repeat from * 13 times more, yarn B, 1dc in each next 3 sts, yarn A, 1 dc in next st, ss into top of first dc to join.

Round 28: yarn B, 1ch, (do not count as st), 1dc into st at base of beg-1ch, 1dc into each next 3 sts, *yarn B, 1dc in each next 4 sts, yarn A, 1dc in each next 4 sts; repeat from * 13 times more, yarn B, 1dc in each next 4 sts, ss into top of first dc to join.

Round 29: yarn A, 1ch (do not count as st), 1dc into st at base of beg-1ch, yarn A, 1dc into each next 3 sts, *yarn B, 1dc in each next 5 sts, yarn A, 1dc in each next 3 sts; repeat from * 13 times more, yarn B, 1dc in each next 4 sts, ss into top of first dc to join.

Round 30: yarn B, 1ch, (do not count as st), 1dc into st at base of beg-1ch, 1dc into next st, yarn A, 1dc into each next 2 sts, *yarn B,

1dc into each next 6 sts, yarn A, 1dc into each next 2 sts; repeat from * 13 times more, yarn B, 1dc into each next 4 sts, ss into top of first dc to join.

Round 31: yarn B, 1ch (does not count as a st) 1dc into st at base of beg-1ch, 1dc into each next 2 sts, yarn A, 1dc into next st, *yarn B, 1dc into each next 7 sts, yarn A, 1dc into next st; repeat from * 13 times more, yarn B, 1dc into each next 4 sts, ss into top of first dc to join.

Round 32: yarn B, 1ch (do not count as st), 1dc into st at base of beg-1ch, *1dc into each st to end of round, changing to yarn C, on the last st, ss into top of first dc to join.

Round 33: yarn C, 1ch (do not count as st), 1dc into st at base of beg-1ch, *1dc into each st to end of round, ss into top of first dc to join.

Repeat the last round twice more and changing to yarn D on the last st, ss into top of first dc to join.

Work the following rounds using the intarsia method, yarns D and E and changing yarn colour on the last st before the colour change:

Round 36 (colour pattern set): yarn D, 1ch (do not count as st), 1dc into st at base of beg-1ch, 1dc into each next 2 sts, *using E, 1dc into each next 3 sts, yarn D, 1dc into each next 3 sts; repeat from * to end of round, ss into top of first dc to join.

Repeat the last round twice more and changing to yarn C, on the last st, ss into top of first dc to join.

Round 39: yarn C, 1ch (do not count as st), 1dc into st at base of beg-1ch, *1dc into each st to end of round, ss into top of first dc to join.

Repeat the last round twice more and changing to yarn B on the last st, ss into top of first dc to join.

Round 42: yarn B, 1ch (do not count as st), 1dc into st at base of beg-1ch, *1dc into each into each st to end of round, ss into top of first dc to join.

Repeat last round once more.

The following rounds create a fold line and edge.

Round 44: 1ch (do not count as st), 1dc into back loop of st at base of beg-1ch, *1dc into back loop of each st to end of round, ss into top of first dc to join.

Repeat last round once more.

Fasten off,

Making up

Weave in loose yarn ends.

To felt the fabric, see Further Information page 122.

Press and steam the fabric with the increase ridges on either side of the bag on the side edges.

Lightly press the lining fabric and with right sides together fold in half.

Place the bag flat onto the lining fabric, using pencil, draw around the bag 2cm (⅞in) from the side and bottom edges and 7.5cm (3in) from the top edge.

Following the pencil line, cut through both layers of fabric.

To the wrong side of the top edge stitch a 5cm (2in) strip, 2cm (⅞in) from the top edge. With the right sides together

and leaving a 1.5cm (⅝in) seam allowance, stitch side and bottom edges of the two pieces of lining fabric together.

Fold the top seam allowance to the wrong side of the fabric and stitch in place.

Trim and clip the seam allowance.

Place the lining inside the bag, fold the top edge of the bag over and stitch the crochet fabric to the lining.

Through both layers of fabric and interfacing, stitch the magnetic clasp halves to the inside of the bag and the bag handles to the outside.

SKITTLE RUNNER pg. 16

Jane: when placing beads within a fabric made from double crochet (US single crochet) the beads are caught into the work with the wrong side facing you. It is really important that you count your stitches properly and check your work at the end of every row - make sure you keep counting,

Measurements

Finished size approximately 33 x 180.5cm (13 x 71in)

Materials

Yarn

Rowan Cotton Glace: 50g (1¾oz) ball(s)

A	Cadmium 486 (lime green)	10
B	Shoot 814 (bright green)	1
C	Toffee 843 (brown)	1
D	Winsor 849 (teal)	1
E	Bubbles 724 (pink)	1

Other

Debbie Abrahams Beads:
size 6, 500 bead pack(s)

Blue 46	5
Lipstick 207	2

Equipment

3mm (US C-2) crochet hook
2.5mm (US 1/0) crochet hook
Stitch markers, twelve
Knitter's sewing or tapestry needle

Tension

22 sts and 24 rows to 10cm (4in) square over double crochet using 3mm (US C-2) crochet hook.

Special abbreviation

b3dc = 3 bead dc: insert hook into st, slide 3 beads to sit as close as possible to base of the hook, yarn around hook beyond the 3 beads and draw through the stitch, yarn around hook, draw through 2 loops to complete the stitch and secure the beads in place.

Note

One ball of Rowan Cotton Glace will work approximately 56 rows of the Main panel.

Method

Main panel

Thread onto yarn A for each pattern repeat:
*[2 blue, 1 lipstick] twice, [1 lipstick, 2 blue] twice *; repeat from * to * 5 times more.
[2 blue, 1 lipstick] twice, 2 blue, 1 lipstick, [4 blue, 1 lipstick] 3 times, 3 blue, [1 lipstick, 4 blue] 3 times, [1 lipstick, 2 blue] 3 times; repeat from * to * 7 times more.
Using 3mm (US C-2) hook and yarn A, make 50ch.
Row 1: skip 1ch, 1dc into each ch to end of row, turn. (49 sts)
Row 2: working in double crochet throughout, work from Chart, overleaf, starting with row 2, placing beads where indicated, turn. Continue to work from Chart, placing beads on WS rows, until 12 pattern repeats have been completed.
Repeat chart rows 1–3 once more.
Fasten off.
Using yarn B, work surface crochet between beads using the photograph and Chart as a guide.

Side border (both alike)

Place a marker in line with the beginning of each of the pattern repeats along the side edge.
With RS facing, using 2.5mm (US 1/0) hook and yarn A, join in yarn.
Row 1: work 32 evenly spaced dc between the markers (384 sts), work 1dc changing to yarn B on the final step of the st, turn. (385 sts)
Row 2: yarn B, 1ch (do not count as st), 1dc into each st to end of row, changing to yarn C on the last st, turn.
Row 3: yarn C, 1ch (do not count as st), 1dc into each st to end of row, turn.
Row 4: 1ch (do not count as st), 1dc into st at base of beg-1ch, *1htr into next st, 1tr into next st, 3dtr into next st, 1tr into next st, 1htr into next st, 1dc into next st; repeat from * to end of row, changing to yarn A on the last st, turn. (513 sts)
Row 5: yarn A, 1ch (do not count as st), dc2tog over next 2 sts, 1dc into each next 2 sts, 3dc into next st, 1dc into each next 2 sts, *dc3tog over next
3 sts, 1dc into each next 2 sts, 3dc into next st, 1dc into each next 2 sts; repeat from * to last 2 sts, dc2tog over next 2 sts, changing to yarn B on the last st, turn.
Row 6: yarn B, repeat the last row, changing to yarn D on the last st, turn.
Row 7: yarn D, 4ch (counts as 1dtr), 1dtr into next st, 1tr into next st, 1htr into next st, 1dc into next st, 1htr into next st, 1tr into next st, * dtr2tog over next 3 sts (skipping second st), 1tr into next st, 1htr into next st, 1dc into next st, 1htr into next st, 1tr into next st; repeat from * to last 2 sts, dtr2tog over next 2 sts, turn.

Row 8: 1ch (do not count as st), 1dc into each st to end of row, changing to yarn E on the last st, turn. (385 sts)
Row 9: yarn E, 1ch (do not count as st), 1dc into each st to end
of row.
Fasten off.
Work Side border along other side to match.

End border (both alike)
Thread onto yarn D, 207 blue beads.
With RS facing, using 2.5mm (US 1/0) hook and yarn D, join in yarn.
Row 1: work 71 evenly spaced dc along runner end, turn.
Row 2: 1ch (do not count as st), 1dc into next st, *b3dc into each of the next 69 sts, 1dc into final st.
Fasten off.
Work End border along other side to match.

Making up
Weave in yarn ends.
Block and press using the preferred method, taking care not to damage the beads with excess heat or pressure.

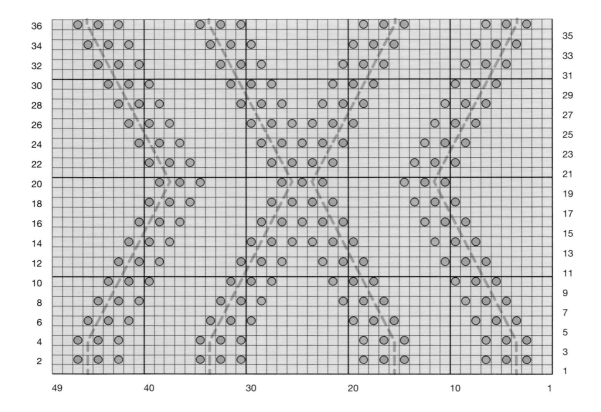

= double crochet, A

= place bead, blue

= place bead, lipstick

= surface crochet, B

WAFFLE CHAIR PAD pg. 52

Jane: this is a deceptively easy design, made from just four crochet pieces. There is a very small area of intarsia so it's a great introduction to this lovely technique. If you're not great at sewing you could always make a rectangular crochet piece to act as the base rather than a fabric one.

Measurements
Finished size approximately
38cm (15¼in) square

Materials
Yarn
Rowan Hand Knit Cotton: 50g (1¾oz) ball(s)

A	Turkish Plum 277 (navy)	1
B	Celery 309 (pale green)	2
C	Pesto 344 (emerald green)	1
D	Florence 350 (orange)	1
E	Rosso 215 (red)	1
F	Slick 313 (pink)	1

Other
Fabric for backing, 100% cotton, ½m (½yd)
of 112cm (44in) wide fabric
Square seat pad, 40 x 40cm (16 x 16in)

Equipment
3.5mm (US E-4) crochet hook
Stitch marker
Knitter's sewing or tapestry needle
Large dressmaker's pins
Sewing needle and matching thread

Tension
18 sts and 20 rows to 10cm (4in) square
over double crochet using 3.5mm (US E-4)
crochet hook

Note
The cushion is made from three panels: one
large crochet panel, which in turn is made from
four identical pieces and two pieces of cotton
fabric

Method
Quarter piece (make 4)
Using yarn A, make 14ch.
Foundation row: skip 1ch, work 1dc into each next 6ch, work 3dc into next ch, 1dc into each ch to end, turn. (15 sts)
Place st marker into the centre st of 3dc. Remove the marker before working the marked st and replace into the centre st after working the marked st.
Row 1: 1ch (does not count as a st) 1dc into each st to marker, [1htr, 1tr, 1htr] into marked st, 1dc into each st to end, turn. (17 sts)
Row 2: 1ch (does not count as a st) 1dc into each st to marker, 3dc into marked st, 1dc into each st to end, turn. (19 sts)
Repeat the last 2 rows once more. (23 sts)
Row 5: repeat row 1, changing to yarn B on the last st, turn. (25 sts)
Row 6: yarn B, repeat row 2, turn. (27 sts)
Row 7: yarn B, repeat row 1, changing to yarn C on the last st, turn. (29 sts)
Row 8: yarn C, repeat row 2, turn. (31 sts)
Row 9: yarn C, repeat row 1, changing to yarn D on the last st, turn. (33 sts)
Row 10: yarn D, repeat row 2, turn. (35 sts)
Row 11: yarn D, repeat row 1, changing to yarn E on the last st, turn. (37 sts)
Rows 12–13: yarn E, repeat the last two rows once more. (41 sts)
Row 14: yarn E, repeat row 2, turn. (43 sts)
Row 15: yarn E, repeat row 1, changing to yarn F on the last st, turn. (45 sts)
Rows 16–17: yarn F, repeat the last two rows once more. (49 sts)
Row 18: yarn F, repeat row 2, turn. (51 sts)
Row 19: yarn F, repeat row 1, changing to yarn E on the last st, turn. (53 sts)
Row 20: yarn E, repeat row 2, turn. (55 sts)
Row 21: yarn E, repeat row 1, changing to yarn D on the last st, turn. (57 sts)
Row 22: yarn D, repeat row 2, turn. (59 sts)
Row 23: yarn D, repeat row 1, changing to yarn F on the last st, turn. (61 sts)
Row 24: yarn F, repeat row 2, turn. (63 sts)
Row 25: yarn F, repeat row 1, changing to yarn B on the last st, turn. (65 sts)
Row 26: yarn B, repeat row 2, turn. (67 sts)
Row 27: yarn B, repeat row 1, changing to yarn C on the last st, turn. (69 sts)
Row 28: yarn C, repeat row 2, turn. (71 sts)

Row 29: yarn C, repeat row 1, changing to yarn A on the last st, turn. (73 sts)

Row 30: yarn A, repeat row 2, turn. (75 sts)

Row 31: yarn A, repeat row 1, changing to yarn B on the last st, turn. (77 sts)

Row 32: yarn B, repeat row 2, turn. (79 sts)

Row 33: yarn B, repeat row 1, turn. (81 sts)

Work the following 4 rows using the intarsia method, yarns B, C and A and changing yarn colour on the last st before the colour change.

Row 34: repeat row 2, yarn B, 1ch (does not count as a st),1dc into each of the next 16 sts, yarn C, 1dc into each of the next 8 sts, yarn A, 1dc into each of the next 16 sts, [1htr, 1tr, 1htr] into marked st, 1dc into each of the next 16 sts, yarn C, 1dc into each of the next 8 sts, yarn B, 1dc into each of the next 16 sts, turn. (83 sts)

Row 35: working the colours set in the last row, repeat row 1, turn. (85 sts)

Row 36: working the colours set in the last row, repeat row 2.

Fasten off.

Making up

Weave in yarn ends.

Block and press using a damp pressing cloth and a warm iron. To make the corners, fold the foundation rows in half, wrong sides together and using mattress stitch, seam the two edges together.

To make a single block, arrange the four pieces so that they form two rows of two pieces. Using mattress stitch, working from the centre out, sew one edge of a piece to its neighbour's edge so that seam is on the inside.

To attach the backing fabric to the crocheted fabric, see Further Information page 122.

Jane: the floor cushion is made by working strips of chevron crochet in one colour at a time. These are then joined on the reverse side of the work by a contrasting yarn and a row of double crochet (US single crochet), the colour of which shows through to the front and creates a really nice feature.

Measurements

Finished size approximately 70 x 70cm (27½ x 27½in)

Materials

Yarn

Rowan Wool Cotton DK: 50g (1¾oz) ball(s)

A	Elf 946 (green)	9
B	Antique 900 (cream)	9
C	Café 985 (orange)	2

Other

Square cushion pad, 76 x 76cm (30 x 30in)

Equipment

4mm (US G-6) crochet hook
Knitter's sewing or tapestry needle

Tension

14–15 sts and 20 rows to 10cm (4in) square over double crochet using 4mm (US G-6) crochet hook

Note

The cushion is made up of strips of alternating colours, which are joined together.
Make 10 strips using yarn A and 10 strips using yarn B.

Method

Strip A (make 10)

Using yarn A, make 177ch.

Foundation row (RS): skip 1ch, 2dc into next ch, *1dc into each next 11 ch, skip 2ch, 1dc into each next 11 ch, 3dc into next ch; repeat from * 5 times more, 1dc into each next 11 ch, skip 2ch, 1dc into each next 11 ch, 2dc into final ch, turn. (176 sts)

Row 1: 1ch (do not count as st) 2dc into next st, *1dc into each next 11 sts, skip 2 sts, 1dc into each next 11 sts, 3dc into next st; repeat from * 5 times more, 1dc into each next 11 sts, skip 2 sts, 1dc into each next 11 sts, 2dc into final st, turn.

Repeat the last row 8 more times.

Fasten off.

Strip B (make 10)

Using yarn B, make 177ch.

Work as Strip A.

Making up

Weave in yarn ends.

Block and press using a damp pressing cloth and a warm iron.

With the wrong side facing and using yarn C, join alternating Strips A and B, work double crochet, matching stitch for stitch, along the final row of one strip to foundation row of the next strip. Using the same method, join the final row of the last strip to the foundation row of the first strip to create a tube.

Using mattress stitch, sew one side seam, insert cushion pad and sew the remaining side seam.

KICKER BLANKET pg. 40

Jane: this large bed blanket is made from a repeat of just 2 squares, which, when sewn together in the correct order can create the appearance of a much more complicated design. When working a colour change in the round you will achieve a really neat join if you fasten off at the end of each round and rejoin in a different place.

Measurements
Finished size approximately 172.5 x 172.5cm (68 x 68in)

Materials
Yarn
Rowan Creative Focus Worsted:
100g (3½oz) ball(s)

A	Saffron 03810 (yellow)	1
B	Syrah 02025 (mauve)	7
C	Deep Rose 02755 (pink)	2
D	Magenta 01890 (dark pink)	2
E	New Fern 01265 (green)	3
F	Golden Heather 00018 (old gold)	9
G	Cobalt 01107 (dark turquoise)	5

Equipment
4mm (US G-6) crochet hook
Stitch markers, four
Knitter's sewing or tapestry needle

Tension
Multi-coloured square, 18cm (7⅛in) square using 4mm (US G-6) crochet hook

Method
Multi-coloured square (make 49)
Using yarn A, make 4ch, ss to join to make ring.
Round 1: 3ch (counts as 1tr) 11tr into ring, ss into top of beg-3ch to join. (12 sts)
Round 2: 3ch (counts as 1tr), skip st at base of beg-3ch, *[2tr, 1dtr] into next st, [1dtr, 2tr] into next st, 1tr into next st; repeat from * twice more, [2tr, 1dtr] into next st, [1dtr, 2tr] into next st, ss into top of beg-3ch to join. (28 sts)
Fasten off, skip 2tr and 1dtr, join yarn B into top of next dtr.
Round 3: yarn B, 4ch (counts as 1dtr), 2tr into st at base of beg-4ch, 1tr into each next 5 sts, *[2tr, 1dtr] into next st, [1dtr, 2tr] into next st, 1tr each next 5 sts; repeat from * to final st, [2tr,1dtr] into next st, ss into top of beg-4ch to join. (44 sts)
Fasten off, skip 2tr and 1dtr, join yarn C into top of next dtr.
Round 4: yarn C, 4ch (counts as 1dtr), 2tr into st at base of beg-4ch, 1tr into each next 9 sts, *[2tr, 1dtr] into next st, [1dtr, 2tr] into next st, 1tr each next 9 sts; repeat from * to final st, [2tr,1dtr] into next st, ss into top of beg-4ch to join. (60 sts)
Fasten off, skip 2tr and 1dtr, join yarn D into top of next dtr.
Round 5: yarn D, 4ch (counts as 1dtr), 2tr into st at base of beg-4ch, 1tr into each next 13 sts, * [2tr, 1dtr] into next st, [1dtr, 2tr] into next st, 1tr each next 13 sts; repeat from * to final st, [2tr,1dtr] into next st, ss into top of beg-4ch to join. (76 sts)
Fasten off, skip 2tr and 1dtr, join yarn E into top of next dtr.
Round 6: yarn E, 4ch (counts as 1dtr), 2tr into st at base of beg-4ch, 1tr into each next 17 sts, *[2tr,1dtr] into next st, [1dtr, 2tr] into next st, 1tr each next 17 sts; repeat from * to final st, [2tr,1dtr] into next st, ss into top of beg-4ch to join. (92 sts)
Place st marker into sp between the 2 dtr sts at each corner.
Using F join yarn into marked sp.
Round 7: yarn F, 1ch (do not count as st), 3dc into same sp, 1dc into each next 23 sts, *3dc into next marked sp, 1dc into each next 23 sts; repeat from * to end, ss into first dc to join. (100 sts)
Round 8: ss into next st, 1ch (do not count as st), 3dc into next st, 1dc into each next 24 sts, *3dc into next st, 1dc into each next 24 sts; repeat from * working last dc into same st as ss at beginning of round, to end, ss into first dc to join. (108 sts)
Fasten off.

Divided square (make 36)

Using yarn B, make 2ch.

Row 1: 3dc into 2nd ch from hook, turn. (3 sts)

Row 2: 1ch (do not count as st), 2dc into next st, 1dc into next st, 2dc into next st, turn. (5 sts)

Rows 3–5: 1ch (do not count as st), 2dc into next st, 1dc into each st until 1 st rem, 2dc into next st, turn. (11 sts)

Row 6: 1ch (do not count as st),1dc into each st to end of row, turn.

Rows 7–18: repeat the last 4 rows, 3 times more, turn. (29 sts)

Rows 19–20: repeat rows 3–4, once more, turn. (33 sts)

Row 21: 1ch (do not count as st), 2dc into next st, 1dc into each st until last st, 2dc into next st, changing to yarn F on the last st and leaving a 30cm (12in) tail of yarn F, turn. (35 sts) Do not break off yarn B.

Rows 22–23: yarn F, 1ch (do not count as st), 1dc into each st to end, turn.

Rows 24: yarn F, 1dc into each st to end, changing to yarn G on the last st and leaving a 30cm (12in) tail of yarn F tail, 300cm (120in) tail of yarn G tail, turn.

Row 25 (RS): yarn G, 1ch (do not count as st), 1dc into each st to end, turn.

Row 26: 1ch (does not count as 1dc), skip 1 st, 1dc into each st to last 2 sts, dc2tog over next 2 sts, turn. (33 sts)

Rows 27–28: repeat row 26, turn. (29 sts)

Row 29: 1ch, 1dc into each st to end, turn.

Rows 30–41: repeat the last 4 rows, 3 times more, turn. (11 sts)

Rows 42–45: repeat row 26, 4 times more, turn. (3 sts)

Row 46 (WS): 1ch, dc3tog.

Fasten off.

Edging

Round 1 (RS): using tail end of yarn G, work 22dc along first side edge, 3dc into top of dc3tog, 22dc along second side edge, changing to yarn F on the last st using attached yarn F, work 3dc into first st of central row, changing to yarn B on the last st using attached yarn B, work 22dc along third side edge, 3dc into ch at beginning of piece, 22dc along second side edge, changing to yarn F on the last st using attached yarn F, work 3dc into last st of central row, ss to first dc to join. (100 sts)

Fasten off.

Place st marker into the centre st of corner 3dc sts.

Join yarn F into marked corner st.

Round 2: 1ch (does not count as a st), *3dc into marked st, 1dc into each st to next marker; repeat from * to end of round, ss to first dc to join. (108 sts)

Fasten off.

Mauve triangle (make 12)
Using yarn B, make 2ch.
Work as for Divided square until row 23.
Edging
Row 1 (RS): 1ch (do not count as st), 2dc into side of last
row, changing to yarn B on the last st work 22dc along first
side edge, 3dc into top of dc3tog, 22dc along second side
edge, changing to yarn F on the last st using attached yarn
F, work 2dc into first st of central row.
Fasten off.
Place stitch marker into the centre st of corner 3dc.
Join yarn F into top of first dc.
Row 2: 1ch (do not count as st), 2dc into st at base of
beg-1ch, 1dc into each st to marker, 3dc into marked st,
1dc into each st to last st, 2dc into final st.
Fasten off.

Old gold triangle (make 12)
Using yarn F, make 2ch.
Work as for Divided square until row 23.
Work Edging as for Mauve triangle in yarn F only.

Making up
Weave in yarn ends.
Block and press using a damp pressing cloth and
a warm iron.
With the wrong side facing, using the Order of piecing
diagram as reference and yarn F, join pieces by working
double crochet, stitch for stitch, along the piece edges,
working along strip by strip to complete the bed spread.
Block and press.

Order of piecing diagram

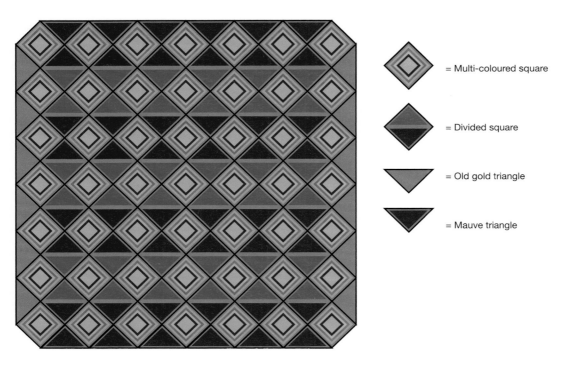

= Multi-coloured square

= Divided square

= Old gold triangle

= Mauve triangle

HOOPLA BOLSTER pg. 28

Jane: the bolster ends are worked in the round and the main part of the cushion cover is made from simple crochet squares that are sewn together. There are a lot of yarn ends to sew in so it's a good idea to do this as you work. Try to sew yarn ends across their matching crochet fabric on the reverse side of the work so that they don't show through to the front.

Measurements
Finished size approximately 40 x 22.5cm (16 x 9in)

Materials
Yarn
Rowan Wool Cotton DK: 50g (1¾oz) ball(s)

A	Wind Break 984 (purple)	3
B	Elf 946 (green)	2

Rowan Revive: 50g (1¾oz) ball

C	Grit 473 (blue/grey)	3

Other
Buttons: 15mm (⅝in)

Purple	5
Ochre	4

Bolster cushion pad, 45 x 20cm (18 x 8in)

Equipment:
4mm (US G-6) crochet hook
3.5mm (US E-4) crochet hook
Knitter's sewing or tapestry needle

Tension
Block one, 8cm (3⅛in) square using 4mm (US G-6) and 3.5mm (US E-4) crochet hooks

Method
Block one (make 36)
Using 4mm (US G-6) hook and yarn A, make 2ch.
Row 1 (RS): 3dc into 2nd ch from hook, turn. (3 sts)
Row 2: 1ch (do not count as st), 2dc into next st, 1dc into next st, 2dc into next st, turn. (5 sts)
Row 3: 1ch (do not count as st), 2dc into next st, 1dc into each next 3 sts, 2dc into next st, turn. (7 sts)
Row 4: 1ch (do not count as st), 2dc into next st, 1dc into each next 5 sts, 2dc into next st, turn. (9 sts)
Row 5: 1ch (do not count as st), 2dc into next st, 1dc into each next 7 sts, 2dc into next st, turn. (11 sts)
Row 6: 1ch (does not count as a st), 1dc into each st to end of row, turn.
Row 7: 1ch (do not count as st), 2dc into next st, 1dc into each next 9 sts, 2dc into next st, turn. (13 sts)
Row 8: 1ch (do not count as st), 2dc into next st, 1dc into each next 11 sts, 2dc into next st, turn. (15 sts)
Row 9: 1ch (do not count as st), 2dc into next st, 1dc into each next 13 sts, 2dc into next st, turn. (17 sts)
Row 10: 1ch (does not count as a st), 1dc into each st to end of row, changing to yarn C on the last st, turn.
Using 3.5mm (US E-4) hook.
Row 11: yarn C, 1ch (does not count as a st), 1dc into each st to end of row, turn.
Row 12: 1ch (does not count as 1dc), skip 1 st, 1dc into each st to last 2 sts, dc2tog over next 2 sts, turn. (15 sts)
Rows 13–14: repeat row 12, turn. (11 sts)
Row 15: 1ch (does not count as a st), 1dc into each st to end of row, turn.
Rows 16–19: repeat row 12, turn. (3 sts)
Row 20 (WS): 1ch, dc3tog.
Fasten off.

Block two (make 18)
Using 4mm (US G-6) hook and yarn B, make 2ch.
Work as for Block one using yarn B in place of yarn A.

Bolster end one

Using 3.5mm (US E-4) hook and yarn C, make 4ch, join with a ss to form a ring.

Round 1: 3ch (counts as 1tr), 11tr into ring, ss into top of beg-3ch to join. (12 sts)

Round 2: 3ch (counts as 1tr), 1tr into st at base of beg-3ch, 2tr into each st to end of round, ss into top of beg-3ch to join. (24 sts)

Round 3: yarn A, 3ch (counts as 1tr), 1tr into st at base of beg-3ch, 1tr into next st, *2tr into next st, 1tr into next st; repeat from * to end of round, changing to yarn A on the last st, ss into top of beg-3ch to join. (36 sts)
Using 4mm (US G-6) hook.

Round 4: yarn A, 3ch (counts as 1tr), 1tr into st at base of beg-3ch, 1tr into each next 2 sts, *2tr into next st, 1tr into each next
2 sts; repeat from * to end of round, changing to yarn B on the last st, ss into top of beg-3ch to join. (48 sts)

Round 5: yarn B, 3ch (counts as 1tr), 1tr into st at base of beg-3ch, 1tr into each next 3 sts, *2tr into next st, 1tr into each next 3 sts; repeat from * to end of round, changing to yarn C on the last st, ss into top of beg-3ch to join. (60 sts)
Using 3.5mm (US E-4) hook.

Round 6: yarn C, 3ch (counts as 1tr), 1tr into st at base of beg-3ch, 1tr into each next 4 sts, *2tr into next st, 1tr into each next
4 sts; repeat from * to end of round, changing to yarn A on the last st, ss into top of beg-3ch to join. (72 sts)
Using 4mm (US G-6) hook.

Round 7: yarn A, 3ch (counts as 1tr), 1tr into st at base of beg-3ch, 1tr into each next 5 sts, *2tr into next st, 1tr into each next
5 sts; repeat from * to end of round, ss into top of beg-3ch to join. (84 sts)

Round 8: 3ch (counts as 1tr), 1tr into st at base of beg-3ch, 1tr into each next 6 sts, *2tr into next st, 1tr into each next 6 sts; repeat from * to end of round, ss into top of beg-3ch to join. (96 sts)

Round 9: 1ch (do not count as st), 1dc into each st to end of round.
Fasten off.

Bolster end two

Using 3.5mm (US E-4) hook and yarn C, make 4ch, join with a ss to form a ring.

Work as for Bolster end one until the end of round 7.

Round 8: 3ch (counts as 1tr), 1tr into st at base of beg-3ch, 1tr into each next 6 sts, *2tr into next st, 1tr into each next 6 sts; repeat from * to end of round, changing to yarn C on the last st, ss into top of beg-3ch to join. (96 sts)
Using 3.5mm (US E-4) hook.

Round 9: yarn C, 1ch (do not count as st), 1dc into each st to end of round.
Fasten off.

Making up

Weave in yarn ends.

Block and press using a damp pressing cloth and a warm iron. Using the Order of piecing diagram as a guide, join the blocks using mattress stitch.

Button band

With RS facing of block row 1 on the Order of piecing diagram, using 3.5mm (US E-4) hook and yarn C, join in yarn.

Row 1: work 73 evenly spaced dc along edge, turn.

Row 2: 1ch (do not count as st), 1dc into each st to end of row, turn.

Repeat the last row 3 times more.

Fasten off.

Buttonhole band

With RS facing of block row 9 on the Order of piecing diagram, using 4mm (US G-6) hook and yarn B, join in yarn.

Row 1: work 73 evenly spaced dc along edge, turn.

Row 2: 1ch, (do not count as st), 1dc into each st to end.

Row 3: (buttonhole row) 1ch, (do not count as st), 1dc into each next 7 sts, 3ch, skip 3 dc, *1dc into each next 4 sts, 3ch, skip 3 dc, repeat from * 7 times more, 1dc into each next 7 sts, turn

Row 4: 1ch, (do not count as st), 1dc into each next 7 sts, 3dc into next ch-sp, *1dc into each next 4sts, 3dc into next ch-sp; repeat from * 7 times more, 1dc into each next 7 sts, turn.

Row 5: 1ch, (do not count as st), 1dc into each st to end. Fasten off.

Place Bolster end one to the edge to the right of the Order of piecing diagram; Bolster end two to the edge to the left of the Order of piecing diagram.

Pin bolster ends to the fabric of blocks, overlapping the Buttonhole band over the Button band by 12mm (½in) and easing the fabric as required. Using matching yarn, stitch bolster ends in place using sewing stitch of choice.

Attach buttons to Button band to align with buttonholes.

Stitch Buttonhole band into place.

Order of piecing diagram

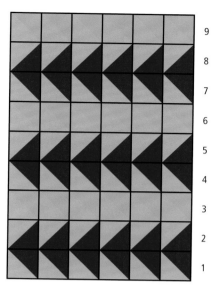

 = Block one

 = Block two

Jane: beaded crochet is really easy and so effective. The beads in this project are worked into the final step of the treble crochet (US double crochet) stitch and are placed when the reverse side of the work is facing you. Make sure you have enough beads threaded on at the beginning of each row as it can be really frustrating to run out! The back of the cover is worked in beaded stripes and the front features beaded fans.

Measurements

Finished size approximately 27.5 x 21cm
(11 x 8¼in)

Materials

Yarn

Rowan Wool Cotton 4ply: 50g (1¾oz) ball(s)

A	Flower 485 (pink)	1
B	Leaf 491 (pale green)	1
C	Marine 495 (navy)	1
D	Violet 490 (lilac)	1

Other

Debbie Abrahams Beads:
size 6, 500 bead pack(s)

Lime green 48	1
Amethyst 41	1

Buttons: 17mm (⅝in)

Pink	6

Equipment

2.5mm (US 1/0) crochet hook
Knitter's sewing or tapestry needle

Tension

21 sts and 15 rows to 10cm (4in) square over Back, striped stitch pattern, using 4mm (US 1/0) crochet hook, with the first counted row, a row of beaded trebles.

Special abbreviation

btr = beaded treble: yarn around hook, insert hook into st, yarn around hook and draw through the stitch, yarn around hook, draw through 2 loops, slide bead to sit as close as possible to base of the hook, yarn around hook beyond the bead and draw through 2 loops to complete the stitch and secure the bead in place.

Method

Back

Thread: 180 lime green beads onto yarn B; 180 amethyst beads onto yarn D.

Using yarn A, make 62ch.

Foundation row: skip 1ch, 1dc into each ch to end, changing to yarn B on the last st, turn. (61 sts)

Row 1 (WS): yarn B, 3ch (counts as 1tr), *1btr into next st, 1tr into next st; repeat from * to end, changing to yarn C on the last st, turn.

Row 2: yarn C, 1ch (do not count as st), 1dc into each st to end of row, changing to yarn D on the last st, turn.

Row 3: yarn D, 3ch (counts as 1tr), *1btr into next st, 1tr into next st; repeat from * to end, changing to yarn A on the last st, turn.

Row 4: yarn A, 1ch (do not count as st), 1dc into each st to end of row, changing to yarn B on the last st, turn.

Repeat the last 4 rows 5 times more. (24 rows)

Do not change yarn colour at the end of the last row.

Working in yarn A only.

Row 25: 3ch (counts as 1tr), 1tr into each st to end, turn.

Row 26: 1ch (do not count as st), 1dc into each st to end of row, turn.

Repeat the last 2 rows, twice more.

Row 31: 1ch (do not count as st), 1dc into front loop of each st to end of row, turn.

Flap

Row 32: 1ch (do not count as st), 1dc into remaining top loop of each st of row 30, to end of row, to create a ridge, ss to beginning of row 31, turn.

Row 33: 3ch (counts as 1tr), working into the sts on row 32 only, 1tr into each st to end, turn.

Row 34: 1ch (do not count as st), 1dc into each st to end of row, turn.

Repeat the last 2 rows, 3 times more.

Fasten off.

Front

Thread for each pattern repeat: 48 lime green beads onto yarn B; 49 amethyst beads onto yarn D.

Using yarn A, make 62ch.

Foundation row: skip 1ch, 1dc into each ch to end, changing to yarn B on the last st, turn. (61 sts)

Row 1 (WS): yarn B, 3ch (counts as 1tr), 3btr into next st, skip 2 sts, 1dc into each next 3 sts, *skip 2 sts, 7btr into next st, skip 2 sts, 1dc into each next 3 sts; repeat from * 5 times more, skip 2 sts, 3btr into next st, 1tr into next st, changing to yarn C on the last st, turn.

Row 2: yarn C, 1ch, 2dc into st at base of beg-1ch, 1dc into next st, *3ch, work a cluster of 7tr over next 7 sts, 3ch, 1dc into each next 3 sts; repeat from * 5 times more, 3ch, work a cluster of 7tr over next

7 sts, 3ch, 1dc into next st, 2dc into top of tch, changing to yarn D on the last st, turn.

Row 3: yarn D, 1ch, 1dc into each next 3 sts, *skip 3ch, 7btr into next st (closing st of cluster on the previous row), skip 3ch, 1dc into each next 3 sts; repeat from * to end of row, changing to yarn A on the last st, turn.

Row 4: yarn A, 3ch, skip st at base of beg-3ch, work a cluster of 4tr over next 4 sts, 3ch, *1dc into each next 3 sts, 3ch, work a cluster of 7tr over next 7 sts, 3ch; repeat from * 5 times more, 1dc into each next 3 sts, 3ch, work a cluster of 5tr over next 5 sts, changing to yarn B on the last st, turn.

Row 5: yarn B, 3ch (counts as 1tr), 3btr into st at base of beg-3ch, skip 3ch, 1dc into each next 3 sts, *skip 3ch, 7btr into next st (closing st of cluster on the previous row), skip 3ch, 1dc into each next 3 sts; repeat from * 5 times more, skip 3ch, 3btr into next st, 1tr into same st, changing to yarn C on the last st, turn.

Repeat the last 4 rows 3 times more.

Repeat rows 2–3 once more.

Break off all yarns, working in yarn A only.

Row 21: 1ch, (does not count as a st) 1dc into each st to end, turn. (73 sts)

Row 22 (buttonhole row) (WS): 3ch (counts as 1tr) tr2tog over next 2 sts, 1htr into each next 2 sts, 1dc into each next 3 sts, *1htr into next st, 1tr into next st, skip 3 sts, 1tr into next st, 1htr into next st, 1dc into each next 3 sts; repeat from * 5 times more, 1htr into each next 2 sts, tr2tog over next 2 sts, 1tr into top of tch, turn. (53 sts)

Row 23: 1ch (does not count as a dc), 1dc into each next 9 sts, *1dc into sp between 2tr, 1dc into each next 7 sts; repeat from * 5 times more, 1dc into each st to end. (59 sts)

Fasten off.

Making up
Weave in yarn ends.
Block and press using the preferred method, taking care not to damage the beads with excess heat or pressure.
Arrange Front and Back pieces, right side facing outwards, so that the Back flap is folded down under the Front piece.
Sew Front to Back piece so that seam is on the inside.
Attach buttons to Back flap to align with buttonholes.

GIDDY BLANKET pg. 44

Jane: this is one of my favourites! It is made from just one repeated rectangle and the edges of the blanket are finished off with half rectangles. The blocks feature surface crochet which is similar in effect to sewn chain stitch, but is worked with a crochet hook and the yarn held to the reverse of the work.

Measurements
Finished size approximately 143 x 133cm (56¼ x 52⅜in) square

Materials
Yarn
Rowan Felted Tweed DK: 50g (1¾oz) ball(s)

A	Seafarer 170 (dark blue)	9
B	Avocado 161 (bright green)	14

Equipment
3.5mm (US E-4) crochet hook
3mm (US C-2) crochet hook
Stitch markers, four
Knitter's sewing or tapestry needle

Tension
Rectangle block, 17.5 x 12.5cm (7 x 5in) using a 3.5mm (US E-4) crochet hook

Method
Rectangle block (make 83)
Using 3.5mm (US E-4) hook and yarn A, make 12ch.
Foundation row: skip 1ch, 1dc into each ch to end of row, turn. (11 sts)
Row 1: 1ch (do not count as st), 1dc into each st to end of row, turn.
Foundation round: 1ch (do not count as st), 1dc into each next 10 sts, 3dc into next st. Do not turn. Work 2dc into side edge of piece, 3dc into remaining side of first st of foundation ch, 1dc into remaining side of next 9 sts of foundation ch, 3dc into remaining side of next st of foundation ch, work 2dc into side edge of piece, work 2dc into same st as first dc at beg of round, ss to first dc to join. (34 sts)
Fasten off.
Place st marker into the centre st of corner groups of 3dc. Remove the markers before working the marked sts and replace into the centre st after working the marked sts.
** With RS facing, join yarn B, into corner st.
Round 1: yarn B, 3ch (counts as 1tr), 4tr into the same st, 1tr into each st to next marker, *5tr into marked st, 1tr into each st to next marker; repeat from * twice more, ss into top of beg-3ch to join. (50 sts)
Fasten off.
With RS facing, join yarn A, into corner st.
Round 2: yarn A, 2ch (counts as 1dc), 2dc into the same st, 1dc into each st to next marker, *3dc into marked st, 1dc into each st to next marker; repeat from * twice more, ss into top of beg-2ch to join. (58 sts)
Fasten off. ***
Repeat from ** to *** twice more. (106 sts)
Join yarn B, into corner st.
Round 7: yarn B, 2ch (counts as 1dc), 2dc into the same st, 1dc into each st to next marker, *3dc into marked st, 1dc into each st to next marker; repeat from * twice more, ss into top of beg-2ch to join. (114 sts)
Fasten off, leaving a tail end of yarn at least 130cm (51in) long.

Half rectangle block (make 10):
Using 3.5mm (US E-4) hook and yarn A, make 6ch.
Foundation row: skip 1ch, 1dc into each ch to end of row, turn. (5 sts)
Row 2: 1ch (do not count as st), 1dc into each st to end of row. (5 sts)
Foundation round: 1ch (do not count as st), 1dc into each next 4 sts, 3dc into next st. Do not turn. Work 2dc into side edge of piece, 3dc into remaining side of first st of foundation ch, 1dc into remaining side of next 3 sts of foundation ch, 3dc into remaining side of next st of foundation ch, work 2dc into side edge of piece, work 2dc into same st as first dc at beg of round, ss to first dc to join. (22 sts)
Fasten off.

Place st marker into the centre st of corner groups of 3dc.
Remove the markers before working the marked sts and
replace into the centre st after working the marked sts.
The following rows are partial rounds, working along 3 sides
of the rectangle.
With RS facing, join yarn B, into next corner st.
Row 1: yarn B, 3ch (counts as 1tr),1tr into each st to next
marker, *5tr into marked st, 1tr into each st to next marker;
repeat from * once more, 1tr into marked st. (26 sts)
Fasten off. Do not turn.
**Join yarn A, into the top of the beg-3ch of the previous row.
Row 2: yarn A, 2ch (counts as 1dc), 1dc into each st to next
marker, *3dc into marked st, 1dc into each st to next marker;
repeat from * once more, 1dc into marked st. (30 sts)
Fasten off. Do not turn.
Join yarn B, into the top of the beg-2ch of the previous row.
Row 3: yarn B, 3ch (counts as 1tr) 1tr into each st to next
marker, * 5tr into marked st, 1tr into each st to next marker;
repeat from * once more, 1tr into marked st. (38 sts)
Fasten off.***
Repeat from ** to *** once more. (50 sts)
Join yarn A, into the top of the beg-3ch of the previous row.
Row 6: yarn A, 2ch (counts as 1dc), 1dc into each st to
next marker, *3dc into marked st, 1dc into each st to next
marker; repeat from * once more, 1dc into marked st. (54
sts)
Fasten off.
Join yarn B, into the top of the beg-2ch of the previous row.
Row 7: yarn B, 2ch (counts as 1dc) 1dc into each st to
next marker, *3dc into marked st, 1dc into each st to next
marker; repeat from * once more (57 sts), 3dc into marked
st, then continue along 4th edge, 22 evenly spaced dc along
side edge of half rectangle, 2dc base beg-2ch, ss to first dc
to join. (84 sts)
Fasten off.

Making up

Weave in yarn ends – leaving long yarn tail end on each
rectangle.
Block and press using a damp pressing cloth and a warm iron.
Using yarn A and the photograph as a guide, work a line
of surface crochet from the centre block to each corner,
finishing before the last round or row of dc.
Strip one (make 6)
With wrong sides together, using long yarn tail end on each
rectangle and double crochet, join the short sides of eight
Rectangle blocks to create a strip one rectangle block high.
Strip two (make 5)
With wrong sides together, using long tail end on each
rectangle and double crochet, join the short sides of one
Half rectangle block, seven Rectangle blocks, then one Half
rectangle block to create a strip one rectangle block high.
With wrong sides together, starting with Strip one and
double crochet, join alternate strips together.

Edging
Place st marker into the centre st of corner groups of 3dc, at
each of the four corners of the blanket. Remove the markers
before working the marked sts and replace into the centre st
after working the marked sts.
With RS facing, using 3.5mm (US E-4) hook and yarn B, join
in yarn into marked stitch with the long edge of Strip to the
left – working along the long side edge of complete blocks.
Round 1: 3ch (counts as 1tr), 4tr into same st, *[1tr into next
32 sts along the side of one block, 1tr into seam] 7 times,
1tr into next 32 sts along the side edge of the final block,
(first side completed 268 sts); 5tr into next marked st,
[1tr into next 24 sts, skip 1 st, 1tr into seam, skip 1 st]
10 times, 1tr into next 24 sts along side edge of half
rectangle blocks, (second side completed 279 sts); 5tr into
next marked st; repeat from * around omitting the last 5tr,
ss into top of beg-3ch to join.
Fasten off.
Using 3mm (US C-2) and yarn A, join yarn into marked stitch.
Round 2: 2ch (counts as 1dc), 2dc into same st, 1dc into
each st to next marker, *3dc into marked st, 1dc into each
st to next marker; repeat from * twice more, ss into top of
beg-2ch to join.
Fasten off.
Block and press.

CRACKLE CUSHION pg. 56

Jane: this cushion is worked in the round and uses the jacquard method where the yarn colour not in use is carried across the reverse of the work until it is needed again. Jacquard crochet is equivalent to the Fairisle technique within the craft of knitting and, as with it's counterpart, it is important to achieve an even tension, so be careful not to over tighten when carrying the contrast yarn.

Measurements
Finished size approximately 39 (15⅜in) diameter

Materials
Yarn
Rowan Wool Cotton 4ply: 50g (1¾oz) ball(s)

A	Sea 492 (light blue)	1
B	Marine 495 (navy)	3
C	Leaf 491 (pale green)	1

Other
Round cushion pad, 40cm (16in) diameter

Equipment
2.5mm (US 1/0) crochet hook
Knitter's sewing or tapestry needle

Tension
24 sts and 24 rows to 10cm (4in) square over double crochet using 2.5mm (US 1/0) crochet hook.

Special abbreviation
mb = make bobble: WS facing, work 5 incomplete treble crochet stitches into the next st so that 6 loops remain on the hook, yarn around hook and draw through all the loops on the hook.

Note
This project is worked in the round using double crochet and a slip stitch into the first dc to join the round. Do not work into the starting chain at the end of the round.

Method
Front
Using yarn A, make a magic loop or 2ch, work 12dc into loop or 2ch, work 12dc into the ch furthest from the hook, ss to first dc join. (12 sts)
Row 1: 1ch (do not count as st), 2dc into st at base of beg-1ch, 2dc into each st to end, ss to first dc to join. (24 sts)
Row 2: 1ch (do not count as st), 1dc into st at base of beg-1ch, 1dc into each st to end of round, ss to first dc to join.
Row 3: 1ch (do not count as st), 2dc into st at base of beg-1ch, 1dc into next st, *2dc into next st, 1dc into next st; repeat from * to end of round, ss to first dc to join. (36 sts)
Row 4: repeat row 2.
Row 5: 1ch (do not count as st), 2dc into st at base of beg-1ch, 1dc into each next 2 sts, *2dc into next st, 1dc into each next 2 sts; repeat from * to end of round, ss to first dc to join. (48 sts)
Row 6: repeat row 2.
Row 7: 1ch (do not count as st), 2dc into st at base of beg-1ch, 1dc into each next 3 sts, *2dc into next st, 1dc into each next 3 sts; repeat from * to end of round, ss to first dc to join. (60 sts)
Row 8: repeat row 2.
Row 9: 1ch (do not count as st), 2dc into st at base of beg-1ch, 1dc into each next 4 sts, *2dc into next st, 1dc into each next 4 sts; repeat from * to end of round, ss to first dc to join. (72 sts)
Row 10: repeat row 2.
Row 11: 1ch (do not count as st), 2dc into st at base of beg-1ch, 1dc into each next 5 sts, *2dc into next st, 1dc into each next 5 sts; repeat from * to end of round, ss to first dc join. (84 sts)
Row 12: 1ch (do not count as st), 1dc into st at base of beg-1ch, 1dc into each st to end of round, ss to first dc to join, changing to yarn B on the ss.
Do not cut yarn A.
Row 13: yarn B, 1ch (do not count as st), 2dc into st at base of beg-1ch, 1dc into each next 6 sts, *2dc into next st, 1dc into each next 6 sts; repeat from * to end of round, ss to first dc to join, changing to yarn A on the ss. (96 sts)
Work the following rounds using the jacquard method, changing yarn colour on the last st before the colour change and stranding yarn across the back of the work when not in use – weaving in the strand every few stitches.
Row 14: yarn A, and working the Chart from right to left, 1ch (do not count as st), 1dc into st at base of beg-1ch, yarn B, 1dc into each next 7 sts, *yarn A, work 1dc into next st, yarn B, 1dc into each next 7 sts; repeat from * to end of round, ss to first dc to join, changing to yarn A on the ss.

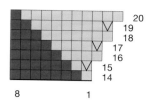

☐ = double crochet, A

■ = double crochet, B

▽ = 2 double crochet stitches
      into the same stitch, A

Rows 15–20: continue to work from Chart, always working from right to left, in the patt set, increasing where indicated.
Row 21: yarn A, 1ch (do not count as st), 2dc into st at base of beg-1ch, 1dc into each next 10 sts, *2dc into next st, 1dc into each next 10 sts; repeat from * to end of round, ss to first dc to join. (144 sts)
Row 22: 1ch (do not count as st), 1dc into st at base of beg-1ch, 1dc into each st to end of round, ss to first dc to join, changing to yarn B on the ss.
Row 23: yarn B, 1ch (do not count as st), 2dc into st at base of beg-1ch, 1dc into each next 11 sts, *2dc into next st, 1dc into each next 11 sts; repeat from * to end of round, ss to first dc to join, changing to yarn C on the ss. (156 sts)
Row 24: yarn C, *mb, yarn B, work 1dc into each next 12 sts; repeat from * to end of round, ss to first bobble to join, changing to yarn B on the ss. (156 sts)
Row 25: yarn B, 1ch (do not count as st), 2dc into st at base of beg-1ch, 1dc into each next 12 sts, *2dc into next st, 1dc into each next 12 sts; repeat from * to end of round, ss to first dc to join, changing to yarn A on the ss. (168 sts)
Row 26: repeat row 22, do not change to yarn B.
Row 27: 1ch (do not count as st), 2dc into st at base of beg-1ch, 1dc into each next 13 sts, *2dc into next st, 1dc into each next 13 sts; repeat from * to end of round, ss to first dc to join. (180 sts)
Row 28: repeat row 26.
Row 29: 1ch (do not count as st), 2dc into st at base of beg-1ch, 1dc into each next 14 sts, *2dc into next st, 1dc into each next 14 sts; repeat from * to end of round, ss to first dc to join. (192 sts)
Row 30: repeat row 26.
Row 31: 1ch (do not count as st), 2dc into st at base of beg-1ch, 1dc into each next 15 sts, *2dc into next st, 1dc into each next 15 sts; repeat from * to end of round, ss to first dc to join. (204 sts)
Row 32: repeat row 22, ss to first dc to join, changing to yarn B on the ss. (204 sts)

Row 33: yarn B, 1ch (do not count as st), 2dc into st at base of beg-1ch, 1dc into each next 16 sts, * 2dc into next st, 1dc into each next 16 sts; repeat from * to end of round, ss to first dc to join. (216 sts)

Row 34: 1ch (do not count as st), 1dc into st at base of beg-1ch, 1dc into each next 4 dc, *yarn C, make bobble into next st, yarn B, work 1dc into each next 17 sts; repeat from * to end of round, finishing with 1dc into each final 12 sts, ss to first dc to join. (216 sts)

Row 35: 1ch (do not count as st), 2dc into st at base of beg-1ch, 1dc into each next 17 sts, *2dc into next st, 1dc into each next 17 sts; repeat from * to end of round, ss to first dc to join. (228 sts)

Row 36: repeat row 26.

Row 37: 1ch (do not count as st), 2dc into st at base of beg-1ch, 1dc into each next 18 sts, *2dc into next st, 1dc into each next 18 sts; repeat from * to end of round, ss to first dc to join. (240 sts)

Row 38: repeat row 26.

Row 39: 1ch (do not count as st), 2dc into st at base of beg-1ch, 1dc into each next 19 sts, *2dc into next st, 1dc into each next 19 sts; repeat from * to end of round, ss to first dc to join. (252 sts)

Rows 40–41: repeat row 26.

Row 42: 1ch (do not count as st), 2dc into st at base of beg-1ch, 1dc into each next 20 sts, *2dc into next st, 1dc into each next 20 sts; repeat from * to end of round, ss to first dc to join. (264 sts)

Rows 43–44: repeat row 26.

Fasten off.

Back

Using yarn A, make a magic loop or 2ch, work 12dc into loop or 2ch, work 12dc into the ch furthest from the hook, ss to first dc join. (12 sts)

Work as for Front in yarn A only, omitting the bobbles.

Making up

Weave in yarn ends.

Block and press using the preferred method, taking care not to flatten the bobbles with excess pressure.

With the wrong side facing and using yarn B, join Front and Back, double crochet matching stitch for stitch around the final round seam until 20cm (8in) remains open.

With right sides facing, insert cushion pad and mattress stitch the open side closed.

Jane: the wave pattern within this design is relatively easy, but the edging does present a little bit more of a challenge. When working the triangle pattern within the edging make sure you keep an even tension on the yarn that is being carried and weave it into the work every now and again to avoid snags and loose stitches.

Measurements

Finished size approximately 45.5 x 46.5cm (18 x 18¼in)

Materials

Yarn

Rowan Cotton Glace: 50g (1¾oz) ball(s)

A	Winsor 849 (teal)	2
B	Cadmium 486 (lime green)	2
C	Garnet 841 (mauve)	4
D	Dijon 739 (olive)	1
E	Persimmon 832 (orange)	1
F	Blood Orange 445 (deep red)	1
G	Ochre 833 (sand)	1

Other

Debbie Abrahams Beads:
size 6, 500 bead pack(s)

Green 49	4

Standard (UK) pillow, 48 x 74cm (18⅞ x 29in)

Equipment

3mm (US C-2) crochet hook
Knitter's sewing or tapestry needle

Tension

22 sts and 24 rows to 10cm (4in) square over double crochet using 3mm (US C-2) crochet hook.

Special abbreviation

mb = make bobble: WS facing, work 5 incomplete treble crochet stitches into the next st so that 6 loops remain on the hook, yarn around hook and draw through all the loops on the hook.

Note

For each wave pattern repeat 196 beads are required.

Method

Main panel

Using yarn A, make 198ch.

Row 1: skip 1ch, 1dc into each ch to end of row, turn. (197 sts)

Row 2: 1ch (do not count as st), *1dc into each next 2 sts, 1htr into each next 2 sts, 1tr into each next 2 sts, 1dtr into each next 3 sts, 1tr into each next 2 sts, 1htr into each next 2 sts, 1dc into next st; repeat from * to last st, 1dc into next st, changing to yarn B on the last st, turn.

Row 3: yarn B, 1ch (do not count as st), 1dc into each st to end of row, changing to yarn C on the last st, turn.

Thread 196 beads onto yarn C.

Row 4 (WS): yarn C, 1ch (do not count as st), 1dc into next st, *1bdc into next st, 1dc into next st; repeat from * to end of row, turn.

Row 5: 4ch (counts as 1dtr) *1dtr into next st, 1tr into each next 2 sts, 1htr into each next 2 sts, 1dc into each next 3 sts, 1htr into each next 2 sts, 1tr into each next 2 sts, 1dtr into each next 2 sts; repeat from * to end of row, turn.

Row 6: 1ch (do not count as st), 1dc into each st to end of row, turn.

Row 7: 1ch (do not count as st), *1dc into each next 2 sts, 1htr into each next 2 sts, 1tr into each next 2 sts, 1dtr into each next 3 sts, 1tr into each next 2 sts, 1htr into each next 2 sts, 1dc into next st; repeat from * to last st, 1dc into next st, turn.

Row 8: 1ch (do not count as st), 1dc into next st, *1bdc into next st, 1dc into next st; repeat from * to end of row, changing to yarn B on the last st, turn.

Row 9: yarn B, 1ch (do not count as st), 1dc into each st to end of row, changing to yarn A on the last st, turn.

Row 10: yarn A, 4ch (counts as 1dtr) *1dtr into next st, 1tr into each next 2 sts, 1htr into each next 2 sts, 1dc into each next 3 sts, 1htr into each next 2 sts, 1tr into each next 2 sts, 1dtr into each next 2 sts; repeat from * to end of row, changing to yarn B on the last st, turn.

Row 11: yarn B, 1ch (do not count as st), 1dc into each st to end of row, changing to yarn C on the last st, turn.

Thread 196 beads onto yarn C.

Row 12: yarn C, 1ch (do not count as st), 1dc into next st, *1bdc into next st, 1dc into next st; repeat from * to end of row, turn.

Row 13: 1ch (do not count as st), *1dc into each next 2 sts, 1htr into each next 2 sts, 1tr into each next 2 sts, 1dtr into each next 3 sts, 1tr into each next 2 sts, 1htr into each next 2 sts, 1dc into next st; repeat from * to last st, 1dc into next st, turn.

Row 14: 1ch (do not count as st), 1dc into each st to end of row turn.

Row 15: 4ch (counts as 1dtr) *1dtr into next st, 1tr into each next 2 sts, 1htr into each next 2 sts, 1dc into each next 3 sts, 1htr into each next 2 sts, 1tr into each next 2 sts, 1dtr into each next 2 sts; repeat from * to end of row, turn.

Row 16: 1ch (do not count as st), 1dc into next st, *1bdc into next st, 1dc into next st; repeat from * to end of row, changing to yarn B on the last st, turn.
Row 17: yarn B, 1ch (do not count as st), 1dc into each st to end of row, changing to yarn A on the last st, turn.
Repeat rows 2– 17, 3 times more, work rows 2–3 once more. Fasten off.

Top and bottom borders (both alike)
With RS facing, and yarn D, join in yarn along last row, or remaining side of foundation chain.
Row 1: 3ch (counts as 1tr) 1tr into next st, *1htr into each next 3 sts, 1dc into each next 5 sts, 1htr into each next 3 sts, 1tr into each next 3 sts; repeat from * to end, ending with 1tr into each next 2 sts, turn. (197sts)
Work the following rows using the jacquard method, changing yarn colour on the last st before the colour change and stranding yarn across the back of the work when not in use.
Row 2 (WS): working in double crochet and mb where indicated, work from Chart starting with row 1, turn.
Continue from Chart, until 10 rows have been completed. Fasten off.

Making up
Weave in yarn ends.
Block and press the runner using a damp pressing cloth and a warm iron.
With right sides facing and mattress stitch, sew the side edges together to form a tube.

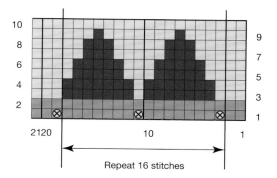

Repeat 16 stitches

 = double crochet, D

 = double crochet, G

■ = double crochet, F

⊗ = mb, make bobble, E

WIGGLE CUSHION pg. 12

Jane: this cushion cover is made by creating a chevron pattern worked in double crochet (US single crochet) throughout. It's a good project for a beginner as it only uses one crochet stitch. When changing yarn shade, remember to do so on the last step of the final stitch on the row so that your turning chain is the correct colour.

Measurements
Finished size approximately 51 x 51cm (20 x 20in)

Materials
Yarn
Rowan Cotton Glace: 50g (1¾oz) ball(s)

A	Garnet 841 (mauve)	4
B	Bubbles 724 (pink)	2
C	Blood Orange 445 (deep red)	2
D	Poppy 741 (red)	2
E	Persimmon 832 (orange)	2
F	Green Slate 844 (pale teal)	1
G	Shoot 814 (bright green)	1

Other
Square cushion pad, 55 x 55cm (21⅝ x 21⅝in)

Equipment
3mm (US C-2) crochet hook
Knitter's sewing or tapestry needle

Tension
22 sts and 24 rows to 10cm (4in) square over double crochet using 3mm (US C-2) crochet hook.

Method
Using yarn A, make 155ch.
Row 1: skip 1ch, 2dc into st at base of beg-1ch, [1dc into each next 7ch, skip 2ch, 1dc into each next 7ch, 3dc into next ch] 8 times, 1dc into each next 7ch, skip 2ch, 1dc into each next 7ch, 2dc into final ch, turn. (154 sts)
Row 2: 1ch (do not count as st) 2dc into st at base of beg-1ch, [1dc into each next 7 sts, skip 2 sts, 1dc into each next 7 sts 3dc into next st] 8 times, 1dc into each next 7 sts, skip 2 sts, 1dc into each next 7 sts, 2dc into top of beg-2ch, turn.
Repeat row 2 throughout working the following stripe sequence.
Rows 3–4: yarn A, changing to yarn B on the last st, turn.
Rows 5–8: yarn B, changing to yarn C on the last st, turn.
Rows 9–12: yarn C, changing to yarn D on the last st, turn.
Rows 13–16: yarn D, changing to yarn E on the last st, turn.
Rows 17–20: yarn E, changing to yarn A on the last st, turn.
Rows 21–22: yarn A, changing to yarn F on the last st, turn.
Rows 23–24: yarn F, changing to yarn G on the last st, turn.
Rows 25–26: yarn G, changing to yarn A on the last st, turn.
Rows 27–34: yarn A, changing to yarn G on the last st, turn.
Rows 35–36: yarn G, changing to yarn F on the last st, turn.
Rows 37–38: yarn F, changing to yarn A on the last st, turn.
Rows 39–40: yarn A, changing to yarn E on the last st, turn.
Rows 41–44: yarn E, changing to yarn D on the last st, turn.
Rows 45–48: yarn D, changing to yarn C on the last st, turn.
Rows 49–52: yarn C, changing to yarn B on the last st, turn.
Rows 53–56: yarn B, changing to yarn A on the last st, turn.
Rows 57–60: using A, do not change yarn colour, turn.
Repeat the colour sequence of the last sequence of rows 1–60, twice more. (180 rows)
Fasten off.

Making up
Weave in yarn ends.
Block and press using a damp pressing cloth and a warm iron.
With the wrong side facing and using yarn A, double crochet, matching stitch for stitch, the final row to the foundation row to create a tube.
With the right facing and using the photograph as reference, position stripe repeat so that the zig zag pattern sits centrally on the front of the cushion cover with the seam to the reverse.
Using mattress stitch, sew one side seam, insert cushion pad and sew the remaining side seam.

KNIT
PATTERNS

Debbie: there are changes in stitch and row tension throughout this design which is caused by the combination of two very different stitches – stocking stitch and star stitch. However, by changing needle size an even width of fabric is maintained so that the completed runner is perfectly rectangular.

Measurements
Finished size approximately: 39 x 142cm
(7⅞ x 56in)

Materials
Yarn
Rowan Cotton Glace: 50g (1¾oz) ball(s)

A	Cadmium 846 (lime green)	1
B	Persimmon 832 (orange)	2
C	Twilight 829 (dark blue)	2
D	Shoot 814 (bright green)	1

Rowan Creative Focus Worsted:
100g (3½oz) ball(s)

E	Charcoal 0402 (dark grey)	1
F	Cream 0100 (cream)	2
G	Magenta 1890 (dark pink)	1
H	New Fern 1265 (green)	1

Other
Debbie Abrahams Beads:
size 6, 500 bead pack(s)

Lipstick 207	1
Mauve 227	1

Equipment:
2.75mm (US 2) knitting needles
3.00mm (US 2/3), 60–80cm (24–40in) circular knitting needles
3.25mm (US 3), 100cm (40in) circular knitting needles, two
4.50mm (US 7) knitting needles
Stitch holder
Knitter's sewing or tapestry needle

Tension
27 sts and 36 rows to 10cm (4in) square over stocking stitch using 3.00mm (US 2/3) knitting needles and Cotton Glace.

Note
The runner is made from two panels that are grafted together. The project in the photograph is long enough for a single bed. Instructions are included at the end of the pattern to make it longer to fit a double bed.

Method
Border
Using 2.75mm (US 2) knitting needles and yarn A, cast on 101 sts.
Carrying yarns up the side of the work.
Join in yarn B.
Rows 1–2: yarn B, knit.
Rows 3–4: yarn A, knit.
Rows 5–16: repeat rows 1–4, 3 times.
Rows 17–18: yarn B, knit.
Break off yarns.

Panel one
Change to 4.50mm (US 7) knitting needles.
Join in yarn E.
Row 1 (RS): yarn E, knit.
Row 2: yarn E, P1, [P3tog leaving sts on LH needle, yrn, purl into same 3 stitches again, P1] repeat to end of row.
Join in yarn F.
Row 3: yarn F, knit.
Row 4: yarn F, P3, [P3tog leaving sts on LH needle, yrn, purl into same 3 stitches again, P1] repeat to last 2 sts, P2.
Rows 5–36: repeat rows 1–4, 8 times.
Join in yarn G.
Rows 37–38: yarn G, work as rows 1–2.
Break off yarns.
Change to 2.75mm (US 2) knitting needles.
Thread 98 lipstick beads onto yarn A; 123 mauve beads onto yarn B.
Rows 39–41: yarn A, knit.
Row 42: yarn A, purl.
Row 43: yarn A, K2, [pb, K1] to last st, K1.
Row 44: yarn A, knit.
Rows 45–50: yarn B, work as rows 39–44.
Rows 51–56: yarn A, repeat rows 39–44.
Break off yarns.
Change to 3.00mm (US 2/3) circular knitting needles.
Starting with a RS, knit, row, work the following stripe pattern on rows 57–86 in stocking stitch, carrying the yarns C and D up the side of the work rather than breaking them off.
Rows 57–64: yarn C. (8 rows)
Rows 65–68: yarn D. (4 rows)
Rows 69–71: yarn C. (3 rows)
Transfer sts back onto other needle.
Rows 72–74: yarn D. (3 rows)
Rows 75–77: yarn C. (3 rows)
Transfer sts back onto other needle.
Rows 78–79: yarn D. (2 rows)

Transfer sts back onto other needle.
Rows 80–82: yarn C. (3 rows)
Row 83: yarn D. (1 row)
Transfer sts back onto other needle.
Rows 84–86: yarn C. (3 rows)
Break off yarns.
Join in yarn B.
Rows 87: yarn B, knit.
Rows 88: yarn B, purl.
Rows 89: yarn B, knit.
Row 90: yarn B, P2, [pb, P3] repeat to last 3 sts, pb, P2.
Rows 91–92: yarn B, repeat rows 87–88.
Row 93: yarn B, K4, [pb, K3] repeat to last st, K1.
Rows 94–95: yarn B, repeat rows 88–89.
Row 96: yarn B, repeat row 90.
Rows 97–98: yarn B, repeat rows 87–88.
Break off yarn.
Change to 4.50mm (US 7) knitting needles.
Join in yarn G.
Row 99 (RS): yarn G, knit.
Row 100: yarn G, P1, [P3tog leaving sts on LH needle, yrn, purl into same 3 stitches again, P1] repeat to end of row.
Break off yarn G. Join in yarn F.
Row 101: yarn F, knit.
Row 102: yarn F, P3, [P3tog leaving sts on LH needle, yrn, purl into same 3 stitches again, P1] repeat to last 2 sts, P2. Join in yarn H.
Row 103: yarn H, knit.
Row 104: yarn H, P3, [P3tog leaving sts on LH needle, yrn, purl into same 3 stitches again, P1] repeat to last 2 sts, P2. Carrying cream and green yarns up side of work, cont as follows:
Rows 105–132: work as 101–104, 7 times.
Rows 133–134: work as 101–102.
Rows 135–136: repeat rows 99–100.
Break off yarns.
Repeat rows 39–98, including all needle size changes and threading of beads.
Repeat rows 99–136, using yarn E in place of yarn H.
Break off yarns.
Leave stitches on a stitch holder or spare needle.

Panel two
Work as Panel one to the end of row 136.
Repeat rows 39–97, including all needle size changes and threading of beads.
Break off yarn B leaving a long tail of approximately 2m (6yds).

Making up
Transfer sts on holder for Panel one onto a 2.75mm needle using yarn B yarn tail, Kitchener stitch or graft the two panels together.
Weave in yarn ends.
Block and press using the preferred method, taking care not to damage the beads with excess heat or pressure.

Edging
Right edge
Using 3.25mm (US 3) circular knitting needles and yarn G, with RS facing, pick up and knit: 10 sts along 18 rows of garter stitch edging; 37 sts along rows 1–38 (section knitted in Cotton Glace); 33 sts along rows 39–98 (section knitted in Creative Focus Worsted), continue in patt set along edge. (333 sts)
Row 1 (WS): yarn G, P3, [P3tog leaving sts on LH needle, yrn, purl into same 3 stitches again, P1] repeat to last 2 sts, P2.
Row 2: knit.
Row 3: P1, [P3tog leaving sts on LH needle, yrn, purl into same 3 stitches again, P1] repeat to end of row.
Row 4: knit.
With WS facing, cast off stitches knitwise.
Left edge
Work as for the Right edge.
Top edge
Using 3.25mm (US 3) circular knitting needles and yarn G, with RS facing, pick up and knit: 4 sts along yarn G edging; 69 sts along Cotton Glace cast-on edge; 4 sts along yarn G edging. (77 sts)
Rows 1–6: knit.
With WS facing, cast off stitches knitwise.
Bottom edge
Work as for the Top edge.
Block and press using a damp pressing cloth and a warm iron

Bed runner for a double bed
You may need an extra ball of yarns A, B, C, D and H.
After completing instructions for Panel one, repeat rows 39–136, followed by rows 39–98 and then rows 99–136 using yarn E in place of yarn H.

SPANGLE BLANKET pg. 46

Debbie: this project is a great way to brush up on your intarsia skills. I chose two yarns to use that are quite different to each other in their style, look and feel. Summer Tweed is flecked and grainy and All Seasons Cotton is smooth and soft. Combined together they enhance the colours and textures of the alternating triangles.

Measurements
Finished size approximately: 150 x146cm
(59 x 57½in)

Materials
Yarn
Rowan All Seasons Cotton: 50g (1¾oz) ball(s)
A	Jacuzzi 239 (blue)	8
B	Hedge 246 (green)	9

Rowan Summer Tweed: 50g (1¾oz) ball(s)
C	Brilliant 528 (pink)	4
D	Summer Berry 537 (red)	6
E	Loganberry 546 (purple)	5

Equipment
4.50mm (US 7) knitting needles
3.75mm (US 5), 100cm (40in) circular knitting needles, two
Knitter's sewing or tapestry needle

Tension
18 sts and 26 rows to 10cm (4in) square over stocking stitch using 4.50mm (US 7) knitting needles.

Note
It is easier to seam the squares in when they have been worked as vertical strips rather than as individual squares. Use the Order of piecing diagram as a guide.

Method
Squares 1–9
Using 4.50mm (US 7) knitting needles, cast on reading row 1 of the Charts from left to right 31 sts, using key of Order of piecing diagram, overleaf, as a guide to colourways. (31 sts)
Beg with a RS row, using the intarsia technique, work all the stitches 1–31, on chart rows 1–42.
With RS facing, cast off stitches knitwise, as colour patt set.

Squares 10–81
Using 4.50mm (US 7) knitting needles, cast on reading row 1 of the Charts from left to right 30 sts, omitting first st, using key of Order of piecing diagram as a guide to colourways. (30 sts)
Beg with a RS row, using the intarsia technique, work stitches 1–30 only, on chart rows 1–42.
With RS facing, cast off stitches knitwise, as colour patt set.

Making up
Weave in yarn ends.
Block and press using a damp pressing cloth and a warm iron.
Using the Order of piecing diagram as a guide and mattress stitch, sew the squares or strips together.

Edging
Right edge
Using 3.75mm (US 5) circular knitting needles and yarn D, with RS facing, pick up and knit 31 sts along the edge of each square. (279 sts)
Row 1 (WS) (increase): K1, inc into next st, knit to the last 2 sts, inc into the next st, K1. (281 sts)
Join in yarn B.
Row 2: yarn B, knit.
Row 3 (increase): yarn B, K1, inc into next st, knit to the last 2 sts, inc into the next st, K1. (283 sts)
Row 4: yarn D, knit.
Row 5 (increase): yarn D, K1, inc into next st, knit to the last 2 sts, inc into the next st, K1. (285 sts)
Join in yarn A.
Row 6: yarn A, knit.
Row 7 (increase): yarn A, K1, inc into next st, knit to the last 2 sts, inc into the next st, K1. (287 sts)
Rows 8–9: yarn D, repeat rows 4–5. (289 sts)
Rows 10–11: yarn B, repeat rows 2–3. (291 sts)
With WS facing and yarn B, cast off knitwise.
Left edge
Work as for the Right edge.

Top edge

Using 3.75mm (US 5) circular knitting needles and yarn D,
with RS facing, pick up and knit 30 sts along the edge of the
first square, [28 sts along of the edge of the next square]
7 times, 30 sts along the edge of the last square. (256 sts)
Work as for Right edge rows 1–11. (268 sts)
With WS facing and yarn B, cast off sts knitwise.

Bottom edge

Work as for the Top edge.
Use yarn ends to stitch corner seams and weave into the
edge seam.
Block and press using a damp pressing cloth and a warm iron.

Chart one

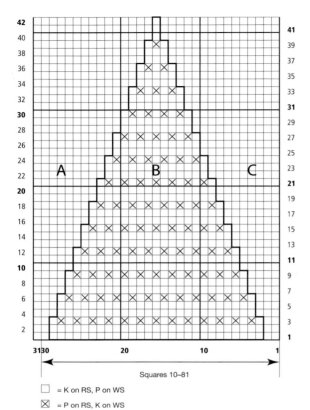

Squares 10–81

☐ = K on RS, P on WS

☒ = P on RS, K on WS

Chart two

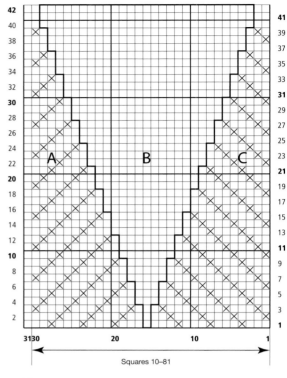

Squares 10–81

☐ = K on RS, P on WS

☒ = P on RS, K on WS

Order of piecing diagram

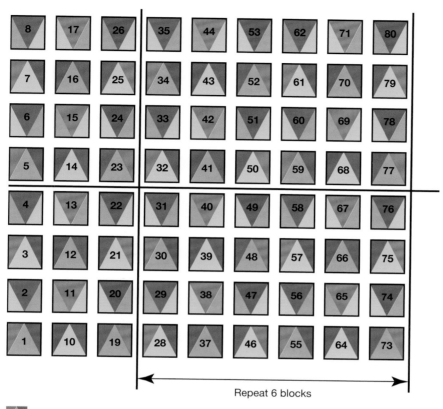

Repeat 6 blocks

Chart one, colourway 1: cast on with yarns C, A and D.

Chart one, colourway 2: cast on with yarns D, B and E.

Chart one, colourway 3: cast on with yarns E, A and C.

Chart one, colourway 4: cast on with yarns C, B and D.

Chart one, colourway 5: cast on with yarns D, A and E.

Chart one, colourway 6: cast on with yarns E, B and C.

Chart two, colourway 1: cast on with yarns B, E and A.

Chart two, colourway 2: cast on with yarns A, C and B.

Chart two, colourway 3: cast on with yarns B, D and A.

Chart two, colourway 4: cast on with yarns A, E and B.

Chart two, colourway 5: cast on with yarns B, C and A.

Chart two, colourway 6: cast on with yarns A, D and B.

ZING BOLSTER pg. 38

Debbie: this beaded striped pattern is easier to knit if you take the yarns up the side edge of the work as this will reduce the number of ends to sew in later on. The circular panels at each end of the bolster are knitted using short-row shaping in a reverse stocking stitch pattern with a textured stitch.

Measurements
Finished size approximately: 40 x 17cm (16 x 6⅝in)

Materials
Yarn
Rowan Cotton Glace: 50g (1¾oz) ball(s)

A	Cadmium 846 (lime green)	2
B	Twilight 829 (dark blue)	2
C	Bubbles 724 (pink)	1

Other
Debbie Abrahams Beads:
size 6, 500 bead pack(s)

White 334	2
Lipstick 207	4

Buttons: 18–20mm (⅝–⅞in)	
Grey	8

Bolster cushion pad, 45 x 17cm (18 x 6⅝in)

Equipment
2.25mm (US 1) knitting needles
3.00mm (US 2/3) knitting needles
Knitter's sewing or tapestry needle
Large dressmaker's pins
Sewing needle, tacking and matching thread

Tension
25 sts and 38 rows to 10cm (4in) square over beaded stocking stitch using 3.00mm (US 2/3) knitting needles.

Note
The yarns not worked are carried up the edge of the knitting. Break off yarns when instructed.

Method
Main panel
Thread for one 30-row pattern repeat: 170 pink beads onto yarn A; 144 white, 56 pink beads onto yarn B. Yarns are broken and re-joined throughout the 30-row pattern repeat, so beads can be threaded onto the yarn as required.
Using 2.25mm (US 1) needles and yarn A, cast on 117 sts.
Row 1 (RS): [K1, P1] repeat to last st, K1.
Rows 2–15: repeat row 1.
Change to 3.00mm (US 2/3) knitting needles.
Row 16 (WS): yarn A, purl.
Row 17: yarn A, knit.
Rows 18–19: yarn A, repeat rows 16–17.
Row 20 (WS): yarn A, P2, [pb pink, P1] repeat to last st, P1.
Join in yarn B.
Row 21: yarn B, knit.
Row 22: yarn B, P3, [pb pink, P1] repeat to last 2 sts, P2.
Row 23: yarn A, knit.
Row 24 (WS): yarn A, P2, [pb pink, P1] repeat to last st, P1.
Row 25: yarn A, knit.
Row 26: yarn A, purl.
Break off yarn A; thread on more pink beads. Join in yarn C.
Rows 27–30: yarn C, work as rows 25–26 twice.
Break off yarn C.
Rows 31–34: yarn B, work as rows 25–26 twice.
Row 35: yarn B, K2, [pb, white, K1] repeat to last st, K1.
Row 36: yarn A, purl.
Row 37 (RS): yarn A, K3, [pb pink, K1] repeat to last 2 sts, K2.
Row 38: yarn B, purl.
Row 39 (RS): yarn B, K2, [pb white, K1] repeat to last st, K1.
Rows 40–41: yarn B, work as rows 16–17.
Break off yarn B and thread on more white and pink beads.
Rows 42–45: yarn C, work as rows 16–17 twice.
Break off yarn C.
Rows 46-225: repeat rows 16–45, including yarn joining and breaks, 6 times more.
Rows 226–235: repeat rows 16–25.
Break off yarn B and use yarn A only for rest of panel.
Row 236 (increase): P58, inc purlwise into next st, purl to end of row. (118 sts)
Change to 2.25mm (US 1) knitting needles.
Row 237 (RS): [K1, P1] repeat to end of row.
Row 238 (WS): [P1, K1] repeat to end of row.
Row 239: [K1, P1] repeat to end of row.
Row 240 (WS) (buttonhole): [P1, K1] twice, P1, [cast off next 3 sts purlwise, work 18 sts in patt set including the last st of cast off in

count] 5 times, cast off next 3 sts purlwise, work rem sts in patt set.

Row 241: [K1, P1] twice, K1, [turn work, cast on 3 sts, turn work, work 18 sts in patt set] 5 times, turn work, and cast on 3 sts, turn work, work rem sts in patt set.

Rows 242–243: repeat rows 238–239.

With WS facing, cast off stitches knitwise.

Circular panels (make 2)

Using 3.00mm (US 2/3) needles and yarn B, cast on 24 sts.

Next row (WS): knit.

Row 1 (RS): P2, K1, [P3, K1] repeat to last st, P1.

Row 2 (WS): K20, wrap the next st, turn.

Row 3: repeat row 1.

Row 4: K16, wrap the next st, turn.

Row 5: repeat row 1.

Row 6: K12, wrap next st, turn.

Row 7: repeat row 1.

Row 8: K8, wrap next st, turn.

Row 9: P2, K1, P3, K1, P1.

Row 10: K4, wrap next st, turn.

Row 11: P2, K1, P1.

Row 12: knit, picking up the wrapped stitches from previous rows and moving them to the back of the work as you knit across the sts.

Row 13: repeat row 1.

Rows 14–23: repeat rows 2–11.

Row 24: K22, wrap next st, turn.

Row 25: K1, [P3, K1] repeat to last st, P1.

Repeat rows 2–25, 7 times more.

With WS facing, cast off stitches knitwise.

Leave a 20cm (8in) length yarn tail.

Making up

To complete the Circular panels, mattress stitch the cast-on edge to cast-off edge.

Using the yarn tail, work a line of running stitch through the edge stitches at the centre of the panel (where there will be a small opening) and draw up the stitches together to close the gap.

Sew one button onto centre of each Circular panel.

Weave in yarn ends.

Block and press using the preferred method, taking care not to damage the beads with excess heat or pressure.

As a temporary join, tack moss stitch edges of Main panel together so that they overlap each other.

Ease and pin the selvedge edge of one Circular panel to the selvedge edge at one end of the Main panel, and using mattress stitch, stitch in place. Repeat for the other Circular panel. Remove the tacking thread.

Attach buttons to align with buttonholes.

NIFTY CHAIR PAD pg. 54

Debbie: the knitted sections of this chair pad cover need to be worked to a very tight tension to create a firm fabric that has limited stretch. Knit the gusset using two circular needles and this will enable you to work comfortably in the round. The back of the cover is made from woven fabric with an envelope opening for easy removal of the pad.

Measurements

Finished size approximately: 38cm (15in) square

Materials

Yarn

Rowan Wool Cotton DK: 50g (1¾oz) ball(s)

A	Pier 983 (bright blue)	1
B	Antique 900 (cream)	2
C	French Navy 909 (navy)	1
D	Elf 946 (green)	1
E	Brolly 980 (yellow)	1

Other

Fabric for backing, 100% cotton, ½m (½yd) of 112cm (44in) wide fabric
Square seat pad, 40 x 40cm (16 x 16in)

Equipment

2.75mm (US 2) knitting needles
2.25mm (US 1), 100cm (40in), circular knitting needles, two
Stitch markers, four
Knitter's sewing or tapestry needle
Large dressmaker's pins
Sewing needle and matching thread

Tension

27 sts and 38 rows to 10cm (4in) square over stocking stitch using 2.75mm (US 2) knitting needles.

Note

The cushion is made from four panels: one large knitted panel; two pieces of cotton fabric; a knitted gusset.

Method

Front panel

Using 2.75mm (US 2) knitting needles, cast on: in yarn A, 19 sts; in yarn B, 9 sts; in yarn C, 9 sts; in yarn B, 27 sts; in yarn C, 9 sts; in yarn B, 9 sts; in yarn D, 19 sts. (101 sts)
Work from the Charts, overleaf, beginning with a RS row on the right-hand page, using the intarsia technique, work chart rows 1–143. Cast off stitches purlwise, with WS facing and keeping colours set by previous row.

Gusset

Using 2.25mm (US 1) circular needle, with the RS facing along the cast-on edge, using yarn E, pick up and knit: 99 sts along the cast-on edge, place marker; 107 sts along the right selvedge edge, place marker; using second circular needle, 99 sts along the cast-off edge, place marker; 107 sts along left selvedge edge, place marker. (412 sts)

Round 1: *[K1, P1] repeat to last st before marker, K1, slip marker; repeat from * to end of round.

Round 2: * K2, [P1, K1] repeat to last st before marker, K1, slip marker; repeat from * to end of round.
Repeat rounds 1–2 until depth of pad.

Next round: knit.
Cast off stitches knitwise.

Making up

Weave in yarn ends.
Block and press using a damp pressing cloth and a warm iron.
To attach the backing fabric to the knitted fabric, see Further Information page 122.

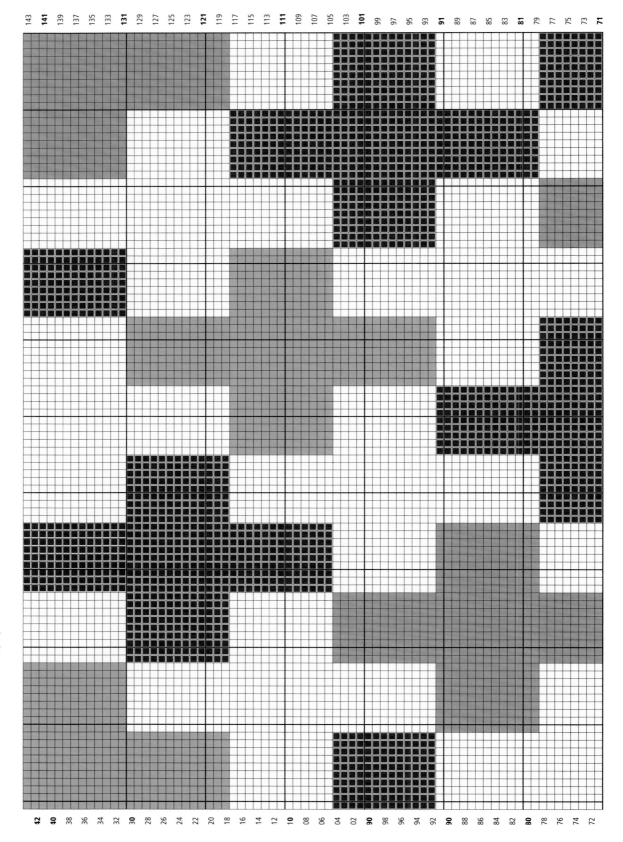

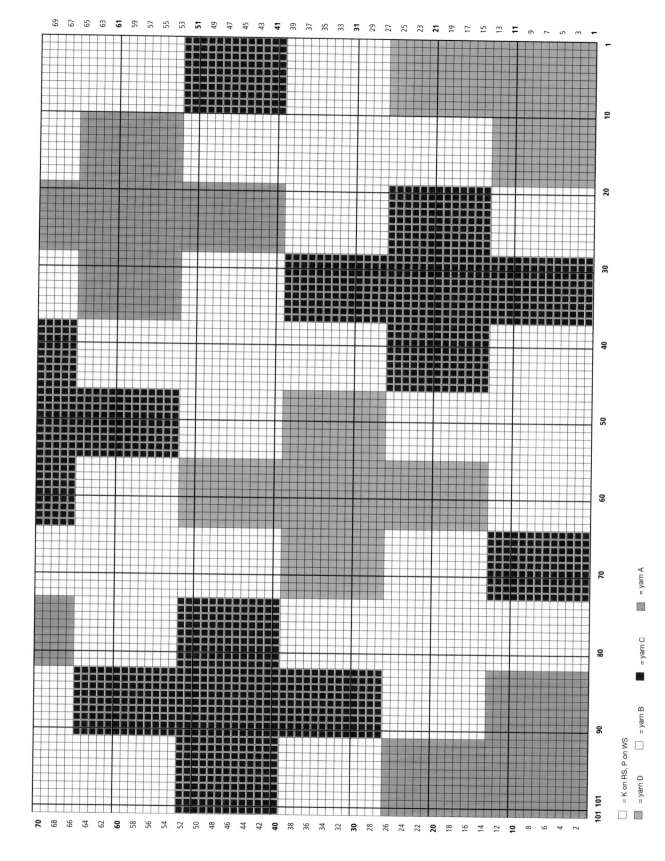

GROOVY CUSHION pg. 26

Debbie: short-row shaping is a fascinating technique and it is the easiest way to knit a circular panel. Wrapping stitches before turning is essential to stop gaps from occurring between the stitches, but the wraps must be picked up and moved to the back of the work when instructed to keep the right-side of the knitting smooth and neat.

Measurements

Finished size approximately:
39 (15⅜in) diameter

Materials

Yarn
Rowan Siena 4-ply: 50g (1¾oz) ball(s)

A	Korma 677 (pale violet)	2
B	Starry 679 (indigo)	2
C	Chilli 666 (red)	1
D	Sorbet 683 (orange)	1
E	Lipstick 680 (pink)	1
F	Madras 675 (yellow)	1

Other
Debbie Abrahams Beads:
size 6, 500 bead pack(s)

Red 38	1

Round cushion pad, 40cm (16in) diameter

Equipment
2.75mm (US 2) knitting needles
Knitter's sewing or tapestry needle

Tension

29 sts and 38 rows to 10cm (4in) square over stocking stitch using 2.75mm (US 2) knitting needles.

Note

This cushion cover is made from two panels that are short-row shaped to create the circular shapes.

Method

Front panel
Thread 96 beads onto yarn A; 108 beads onto yarn B.
Using 2.75mm (US 2) knitting needle and yarn A, cast on 58 sts.
Next row (WS): purl.
Working from Chart one, overleaf, using the intarsia technique, cont as follows:
Row 1 (RS): knit.
Row 2 (WS): purl, (ignoring the beads).
Row 3: K54 sts, wrap next st, turn.
Row 4: purl.
Row 5: K50 sts, wrap next st, turn.
Row 6: purl.
Cont to work from Chart one, wrapping sts where indicated, until chart row 28 is completed.
*Working from Chart two and using the intarsia technique, cont as follows:
Row 1 (RS): knit, picking up the wrapped stitches from previous rows and moving them to the back of the work as you knit across the sts.
Row 2 (WS): purl, (including the beads).
Row 3: K54 sts, wrap next st, turn.
Row 4: purl.
Row 5: K50 sts, wrap next st, turn.
Row 6: purl.
Cont to work from Chart two, overleaf, wrapping sts where indicated, until chart row 28 is completed.
Working from Chart one and using the intarsia technique, cont as follows:
Row 1 (RS): knit, picking up the wrapped stitches from previous rows and moving them to the back of the work as you knit across the sts.
Row 2 (WS): purl, (including the beads).
Row 3: K54 sts, wrap next st, turn.
Row 4: purl.
Row 5: K50 sts, wrap next st, turn.
Row 6: purl.
Cont to work from Chart one, wrapping sts where indicated, until chart row 28 is completed.*
Repeat from * to * 7 times more.
Work 28 rows from Chart two once more, wrapping sts where indicated, until chart row 28 is completed.
Cast off stitches knitwise, with RS facing, using yarn B and picking up the wraps from previous rows and moving them to the back of the work as you cast off.
Leave a 20cm (8in) yarn tail.

Back panel

Thread 96 beads onto yarn A; 108 beads onto yarn B.
Using 2.75mm (US 2) knitting needle and yarn A, cast on
58 sts.
Work as for Front panel, working Chart one as before, but,
working from Chart three, overleaf, instead of Chart two.

Making up

To complete the Front and Back panels, mattress stitch the
cast-on edge to cast-off edge.
Using the yarn tail, work a line of running stitch through the
edge stitches at the centre of the panel (where there will be
a small opening) and draw up the stitches together to close
the gap.

On the Front panel, using yarn A, sew 12 beads along the
seam, positioning them on stitches: 6, 10, 14, 18, 22, 26,
30, 34, 38, 42, 46 and 50.
Weave in yarn ends.
Block and press using the preferred method, taking care not
to damage the beads with excess heat or pressure.
With the wrong side facing and using yarn A, align the
seam and the pattern repeats, and using mattress stitch,
join 7 pattern repeats of the two panels together. Insert the
cushion pad and mattress stitch the opening closed.

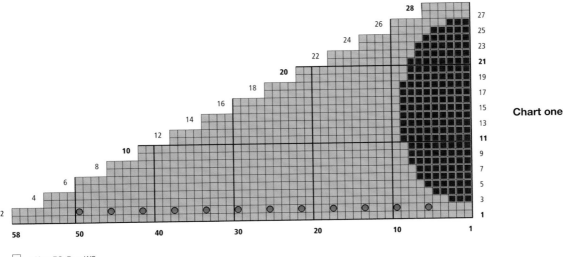

Chart one

☐ = K on RS, P on WS

◉ = pb (place bead) red

▨ = yarn A

■ = yarn B

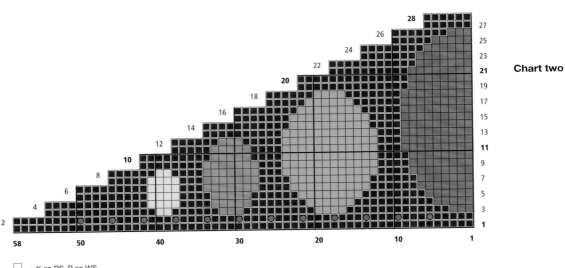

Chart two

☐ = K on RS, P on WS

◉ = pb (place bead) red

■ = yarn B

▨ = yarn C

▨ = yarn D

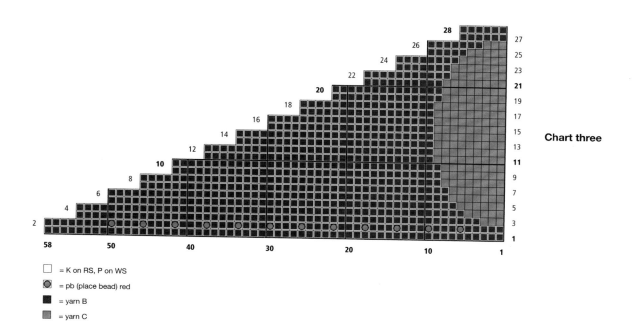

Chart three

☐ = K on RS, P on WS
◉ = pb (place bead) red
■ = yarn B
▨ = yarn C

LOLLY BAG pg. 10

Debbie: I haven't experimented with felting knitting since my days at university, so for me this was a real step back in time. If you have not tried felting before then this is a good place to start. The addition of good quality handles and a lining make this a strong and durable bag.

Measurements
Finished size approximately: 42.5 x 32.5cm (17 x 13in)

Materials
Yarn
Rowan Creative Focus Worsted:
100g (3½oz) ball(s)

A	Charcoal 0402 (dark grey)	1
B	Magenta 1890 (dark pink)	2
C	Cream 0100 (cream)	2
D	New Fern 1265 (green)	1
E	True Purple 1800 (purple)	1
F	Saffron 3810 (yellow)	1

Other
Fabric for lining, 100% cotton, ½m (½yd) of 112cm (44in) wide fabric
Bag handles, sew on purple leather, 71cm (28in)

Equipment
5.00mm (US 8) knitting needles
Knitter's sewing or tapestry needle
Large dressmaker's pins
Sewing needle, tacking and matching sewing and embroidery thread

Tension (before felting)
19 sts and 23 rows to 10cm (4in) square over stocking stitch using 5.00mm (US 8) knitting needles.

Note
The bag is made from three felted panels that are cut and sewn together. Stitches and rows have been added to allow for cutting the pieces to size and for the seam allowance.

Method
Main panel (make 2)
Using 5.00mm (US 8) knitting needles and yarn A, cast on 135 sts.
Starting with a RS row, working in stocking stitch throughout, work in foll stripe patt:
Rows 1–28: yarn A. (28 rows)
Rows 29–36: yarn B. (8 rows)
Rows 37–40: yarn A. (4 rows)
Rows 41–58: yarn C. (18 rows)
Rows 59–66: yarn D. (8 rows)
Rows 67–70: yarn C. (4 rows)
Rows 71–78: yarn E. (18 rows)
Rows 79–86: yarn F. (8 rows)
Rows 87–90: yarn E. (4 rows)
Rows 91–108: yarn C. (18 rows)
Rows 109–116: yarn B. (8 rows)
Rows 117–124: yarn C. (8 rows)
Cast off stitches knitwise.

Base panel
Using 5.00mm (US 8) knitting needles and yarn B, cast on 90 sts.
Starting with a RS row, work 80 rows in stocking stitch.
Cast off stitches knitwise.

Making up
Weave in loose yarn ends.
To felt the fabric, see Further Information page 122.
Press and steam the fabric making sure that the stripes are straight.
The following measurements are approximate and will depend on the finished size of your felted pieces.
From both Main panels, cut a piece 45 x 35cm (18 x 14in). Shape the bottom corners so that the bottom edge is 35cm (14in) wide.
With right sides together, allowing a 1.5cm (⅝in) seam allowance, stitch two panels together along side seams, matching the stripes.
Press the seams open.
For Base panel, trim off the rolled edges and cut a piece 35 x 20cm (14 x 8in).
With right sides together, match centre of each short edge of Base panel with side seams and centre of long edges with centres of bottom edge of Main panels and pin in place – creating a curved seam.
Allowing a 1.5cm (⅝in) seam allowance, sew the two pieces together matching.
Press the seams open.

Cut two small pieces of fabric from the waste knitted fabric.
Stitch the handles in place using embroidery thread, placing
the pieces of waste knitted fabric behind the stitching on
the inside of the bag to add extra strength.

For the lining, fold the lining fabric in half, place the bag on
top of the fabric and cut around bag, leaving an excess of
2.5cm (1in).

With right side together, allowing a 1.5cm (⅝in) seam
allowance, stitch along side and bottom seams.

Carefully clip the curved seams and press the seams open.
Place the lining inside bag, fold the excess fabric along the
top edge between the bag and the lining and stitch in place.

Debbie: the great thing about this project is that the knitting is felted in your washing machine, so the colour joins between the intarsia circles do not have to be perfect, tempting even the most novice colour knitter to have a go. The construction is simple - after the two panels have been felted they are cut to size and sewn together along all four edges, but extra care should be taken to make sure that the stripes match up on the seams.

Measurements

Finished size approximately: 73 x 49cm
(59 x 57½in)

Materials

Yarn

Rowan Creative Focus Worsted:
100g (3½oz) ball(s)

A	Deep Rose 2755 (pink)	2
B	Nickel 0401 (light grey)	2
C	Blue Moor Heather 0791 (warm grey)	2
D	Magenta 1890 (dark pink)	2

Other

A sheet of tissue paper, at least 75 x 52cm
(32 x 20½in)
Cushion pad, 74 x 48cm (29 x 19in)

Equipment

5.00mm (US 8), 80–100cm (32–40in) circular
knitting needle
Stitch markers, two
Knitter's sewing or tapestry needle
Sewing needle and matching thread

Tension (before felting)

19 sts and 23 rows to 10cm (4in) square
over stocking stitch using 5.00mm (US 8)
knitting needles.

Note

The cushion cover is made from two felted
panels that are cut and sewn together. Extra
stitches and rows have been included to allow
for cutting and seam allowance.

Method

Panel one

Using 5mm (US 8) circular knitting needle and yarn A, cast on 180 sts.
Row 1 (RS): knit.
Row 2: purl.
Rows 3–10: repeat rows 1–2, 4 times.
Row 11 (chart row 1) (RS): K10, place marker, working from Chart, overleaf, using the intarsia technique, work right to left, stitches 1–56, [chart stitches 5–56] twice, end Chart, place marker, K10.
Row 12 (chart row 2) (WS): P10, slip stitch marker, working from Chart, using the intarsia technique, work left to right [chart stitches 56–5] 3 times, chart stitches 4–1, end Chart, slip stitch marker, P10.
The stitch markers mark the start and finish of the chart stitches.
Rows 13– 54: keeping 10 sts at each edge as set, work chart rows 3–44.
Rows 55–98: keeping 10 sts at each edge as set, using the Panel one colour diagram overleaf as a guide, work chart rows 1–44: using yarn B in place of yarn A; yarn D in place of yarn B; yarn A in place of yarn C.
Rows 99–142: repeat rows 11–54.
Rows 143–186: repeat rows 55–98.
Rows 187–196: yarn B, work 10 rows in stocking stitch.
Cast off stitches knitwise.

Panel two

Using 5mm (US 8) circular knitting needle and yarn D, cast on 180 sts.
Row 1 (RS): knit.
Row 2: purl.
Rows 3–10: repeat rows 1–2, 4 times.
Rows 11–54: using yarn D in place of yarn A, work rows 11–54 of Panel one.
Rows 55–98: keeping 10 sts at each edge as set, using the Panel two colour diagram overleaf as a guide, work chart rows 1–44: using yarn C in place of yarn A (on the Chart); yarn D in place of yarn B (on the chart); yarn A in place of yarn C.
Rows 99–142: repeat rows 11–54.
Rows 143–186: repeat rows 55–98.
Rows 187–196: yarn C, work 10 rows in stocking stitch.
Cast off stitches knitwise.

Making up

Weave in loose yarn ends.

To felt the fabric, see Further Information page 122.
Press and steam the fabric making sure that the stripes
are straight.

The following measurements are approximate and will
depend on the finished size of your felted pieces.
Make a paper template approximately 75 x 52cm
(32 x 20½in).

With approximately 5 stitches beyond the sided edges of
the template and 3 rows beyond the top and bottom, pin the
template in the centre of each panel and cut out.

With right sides together, allowing a 1.5cm (⅜in) seam
allowance and starting in the middle of one of the short
sides, sew the two pieces together matching the greys and
pinks and finishing half a side length distance from the start
– leaving a gap in the middle of a short side.

Press the seams open.

Trim the seam allowances and cut the corners diagonally
close to the stitching to reduce the seam bulk.

Turn the right sides out, insert the cushion pad and sew the
gap in the short edge closed.

Block and press using a damp pressing cloth and a warm iron.

Chart

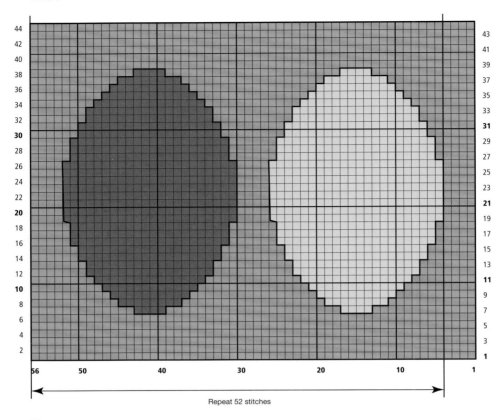

Repeat 52 stitches

 = K on RS, P on WS

= yarn A

= yarn B

= yarn C

Panel one colour diagram

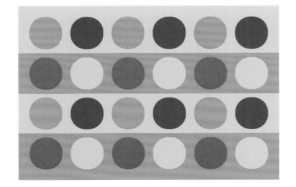

Panel two colour diagram

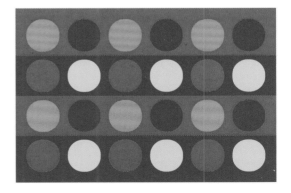

Debbie: the big plus point about working in the round is that there are no seams, so this tablet cover will delight those who do not enjoy sewing up. There is just one seam along the bottom edge, but if preferred this can be crocheted or knitted together instead of sewn.

Measurements

Finished size approximately: 26 x 20cm (10¼ x 8in)

Materials

Yarn

Rowan Handknit Cotton: 50g (1¾oz) ball

A	Violet 353 (lilac)	1
B	Turkish Plum 277 (navy)	1
C	Gooseberry 219 (bright green)	1

Other

Buttons: 25mm (1in)

Green	3

Equipment

3.25mm (US 3), 40cm (16in) circular knitting needle

2.75mm (US 2), 40cm (16in) circular knitting needle

Stitch markers, two

Knitter's sewing or tapestry needle

Tension

22 sts and 33 rows to 10cm (4in) square over textured pattern using 3.25mm (US 3) knitting needles.

Note

The cover is knitted on a circular needle so that side seams are omitted.

Method

Using 3.25mm (US 3) circular knitting needle and yarn A, cast on 112 sts. Place stitch markers on stitches 1 and 56 to indicate where the Front panel starts and finishes.

Ensuring that the stitches are not twisted around the cable, join to work in the round.

Round 1 (RS): knit.

Round 2: *[K1, P1] 3 times, K1, P7; repeat from * to end of round.

Round 3: [K7, P7] repeat to end of round.

Rounds 4–5: repeat rounds 2–3.

Join in yarn B.

Rounds 6–11: yarn B, repeat rounds 2–3, 3 times.

Join in yarn C.

Round 12: yarn C, *P7, [K1, P1] 3 times, K1; repeat from * to end of round.

Round 13: yarn C, [P7, K7] repeat to end of round.

Rounds 14–15: yarn C, repeat rounds 12–13.

Rounds 16–21: yarn B, repeat rounds 12–13, 3 times.

Rounds 22– 61: repeat rounds 2–21, twice more.

Break off yarns B and C.

Change to a 2.75mm (US 2) circular knitting needle and work using yarn A.

Round 62: [P1, K1] repeat to end of round.

Round 63: [K1, P1] repeat to end of round.

Rounds 64–67: repeat rounds 62–63 twice more.

Round 68: keeping patt as set, patt across 5 sts, [cast off next 4 sts, patt across 17 sts including the last st of cast off in count] twice, cast off next 4 sts, patt to end of round.

Round 69: keeping patt as set, patt across 5 sts, [turn work and cast on 4 sts, turn work, patt across 17 sts] twice, turn work and cast on 4 sts, turn work, patt to end of round.

Round 70: [P1, K1] repeat to end of round.

Round 71: [K1, P1] repeat to end of round.

Round 72: [P1, K1] repeat to end of round.

Break off yarn A. Join in yarn C.

Cast off stitches knitwise.

Making up

Weave in yarn ends.

Make a template to the measurements listed above.

To block, insert the template inside the cover, spray it with cold water and leave to dry.

Using mattress stitch, sew the cast-on edges of cover together, so that the seam begins and ends with the markers for Front panel, taking care to match the pattern across the seam.

Attach buttons to align with buttonholes.

MALLOW BLANKET pg. 34

Debbie: the idea behind this design is simple – one block of triangles in one colourway that when joined together with the same block creates another triangular pattern between the blocks. It uses the intarsia technique combined with a simple purl stitch pattern. Why not try it in your own choice of three colours, or be really brave and knit each block in a different colourway? The results could be amazing!

Measurements
Finished size approximately: 92cm (36¼in) square

Materials
Yarn
Rowan All Seasons Cotton: 50g (1¾oz) ball(s)

A	Hedge 246 (green)	8
B	Damson 241 (mauve)	6
C	Cream 178 (cream)	4

Equipment
4.50mm (US 7) knitting needles
3.75mm (US 5), 100cm (40in) circular knitting needles, two
Knitter's sewing or tapestry needle

Tension
18 sts and 26 rows to 10cm (4in) square over stocking stitch using 4.50mm (US 7) knitting needles.

Note
It is easier to seam the squares in when they have been worked as vertical strips rather than as individual squares. Use the Order of piecing diagram as a guide.

Method
Squares 1–6
Using 4.50mm (US 7) knitting needles, cast on: in yarn A, 2 sts; in yarn B, 13 sts; in yarn C, 1 st; in yarn B, 13 sts; in yarn A, 2 sts. (31 sts)
Beg with a RS row, using the intarsia technique, work all the stitches 1–31, on chart rows 1–42.
With RS facing, cast off stitches knitwise, as colour patt set.

Squares 7–36
Using 4.50mm (US 7) knitting needles, cast on: in yarn A, 1 sts; in yarn B, 13 sts; in yarn C, 1 st; in yarn B, 13 sts; in yarn A, 2 sts. (30 sts)
Beg with a RS row, using the intarsia technique, work stitches 1–30 only, on chart rows 1–42.
With RS facing, cast off stitches knitwise, as colour patt set.

Making up
Weave in yarn ends.
Block and press using a damp pressing cloth and a warm iron.
Using the Order of piecing diagram as a guide and mattress stitch, sew the squares or strips together.

Edging
Right edge
Using 3.75mm (US 5) circular knitting needles and yarn C, with RS facing, pick up and knit 32 sts along the edge of each square. (192 sts)
Row 1 (WS) (increase): K1, inc into next st, knit to the last 2 sts, inc into the next st, K1. (194 sts)
Row 2: purl.
Leaving 15cm (6in) yarn tail, break off yarn C, join in yarn B.
Row 3 (increase): P1, inc into next st, purl to the last 2 sts, inc into the next st, P1. (196 sts)
Row 4: purl.
Rows 5–6: yarn B, repeat rows 1–2. (198 sts)
With WS facing, cast off stitches knitwise.
Left edge
Work as for the Right edge.
Top edge
Using 3.75mm (US 5) circular knitting needles and yarn C, with RS facing, pick up and knit 30 sts along the edge of the first square, [28 sts along the edge of the next square] 4 times, 30 sts along the edge of the last square. (172 sts)
Work as for Right edge rows 1–6. (178 sts)
With WS facing, cast off stitches knitwise.
Bottom edge
Work as for the Top edge.
Use yarn ends to stitch corner seams and weave into the edge seam.
Block and press using a damp pressing cloth and a warm iron.

Order of piecing diagram

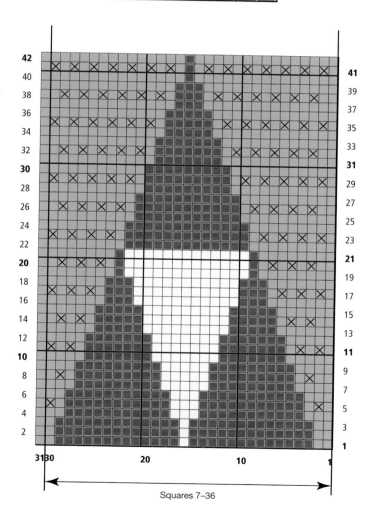

☐ = K on RS, P on WS

☒ = P on RS, K on WS

▨ = yarn A

■ = yarn B

☐ = yarn C

Squares 7–36

PIZZAZZ PILLOW SLIP pg. 42

Debbie: thumb method is the preferred way to cast on for this project so that beads lay nice and neatly along the edge of the knitting. Just make sure that when each bead is placed it is pushed away from you as you put the new stitch on the needle. The stitch will then close up above the bead, securing it firmly in the cast-on edge.

Measurements
Finished size approximately: 49cm (19¼in) square (90cm (35½in) circumference)

Materials
Yarn
Rowan Cotton Glace: 50g (1¾oz) ball(s)

A	Cadmium 846 (lime green)	5
B	Umber 838 (chocolate)	2
C	Winsor 849 (teal)	1
D	Ecru 725 (cream)	2

Other
Debbie Abrahams Beads:
size 6, 500 bead pack(s)

Lipstick 207	2
Blue 46	2
Bronze 601	1

Standard (UK) pillow, 48 x 74cm (18⅞ x 29in)

Equipment
2.25mm (US 1), 80–100cm (32–40in) circular knitting needle
3.00mm (US 2/3), 80–100cm (32–40in) circular knitting needle
Stitch holder or spare circular knitting needles
Knitter's sewing or tapestry needle

Tension
29 sts and 38 rows to 10cm (4in) square over cable and moss stitch using 3.00mm (US 2/3) knitting needles.

Special abbreviation
bco = beaded cast on: slide bead to sit as close as possible to base of the needle, cast on 1 st ensuring that the bead is on the WS of the work (away from you) as you put the cast-on loop onto the needle.

Method
Panel one
Section one
Thread 119 blue beads onto yarn A.
Using 2.25mm (US 1) circular knitting needle, yarn A, the thumb method with beads on ball side; cast on 2 sts, [bco, cast on 1 st without bead] repeat until there are 240 sts.
Next row (WS): purl.
Join in yarn B.
Row 1–4: yarn B, knit.
Row 5: yarn A, knit.
Row 6: yarn A, purl.
Join in yarn C.
Rows 7–10: yarn C, knit.
Row 11: yarn A, knit.
Row 12: yarn A, purl.
Slide the sts along the cable to the other end of the knitting needle.
Change to 3.00mm (US 2/3) circular knitting needle.
Row 13 (WS): yarn B, purl.
Row 14: yarn B, K1, inc into next st, K4, sl 1, K1, psso, K2tog, K4, *inc into each of the next 2 sts, K4, sl 1, K1, psso, K2tog, K4; repeat from * to last 2 sts, inc in next st, K1.
Row 15: yarn B, knit.
Row 16: yarn B, repeat row 14.
Join in yarn D.
Rows 17–20: yarn D, work as rows 13–16.
Rows 21-36: works as rows 13–20, twice.
Slide the sts along the circular needle to the other end of the knitting needle.
Break off yarns A, C, D.
Section two
Thread: 119 lipstick beads onto yarn C; 119 bronze beads onto yarn A; 119 blue beads onto yarn D.
Change to 2.25mm (US 1) circular knitting needle.
Row 37 (RS): yarn C, knit.
Row 38: yarn C, knit.
Change to 3.00mm (US 2/3) circular knitting needle.
Row 39: yarn C, knit.
Row 40: yarn C, purl.
Row 41: yarn C, [K1, pb] repeat to last 2 sts, K2.
Change to 2.25mm (US 1) circular knitting needle.
Row 42: yarn C, knit.
Rows 43–48: yarn A, repeat rows 37–42, including needle size changes.

Rows 49-54: yarn D, repeat rows 37–42, including needle size changes.

Row 55: yarn B, K47 [K2tog, K46] 3 times, K2tog, K47. (236 sts)

Row 56: yarn B, knit.

Break off all yarns.

Section three

Thread onto yarn A: 36 lipstick beads; 36 blue beads. These 72 beads are enough for two repeats across the cable pattern.

Repeat the threading sequence until yarn is full.

Thread additional beads in this sequence, as you need them.

Change to 3.00mm (US 2/3) circular knitting needle and yarn A only.

Row 57: knit.

Row 58 (increase): K1, *[K1, inc into next st purlwise, P1] 4 times, K1, [P1, K1] 6 times, P1; repeat from * to last st, K1. (272 sts)

Row 59: K1, *[P1, K1] 6 times, P1, [P1, K1, pb, K1] 4 times, P1; repeat from * to last st, K1.

Row 60: K1, *[K1, P3] 4 times, K1, [P1, K1] 6 times, P1; repeat from * to last st, K1.

Row 61: K1, *[P1, K1] 6 times, P1, [P1, c3b] 4 times, P1; repeat from * to last st, K1.

Row 62: repeat row 60.

Repeat rows 59–62 until cable section measures approximately 24cm (9½in), ending with row 59 and blue beads.

Next row (WS) (decrease): K1, *[K1, P2tog, P1] 4 times, K1, [P1, K1] 6 times, P1; repeat from * to last st, K1. (236 sts)

Break yarn A leaving a long tail of approximately 2m (6yds).

Leave stitches on a stitch holder or spare needle.

Panel two

Thread 119 blue beads onto yarn A.

Using yarn A, 2.25mm (US 1) circular knitting needle, the thumb method with beads on ball side; cast on 2 sts, [bco, cast on 1 st without bead] repeat until there are 240 sts.

Next row (WS): purl.

Join in yarn B.

Repeat rows 1–56 of Panel one.

Leave stitches on the needle.

Making up

Weave in yarn ends.

Block and press using the preferred method, taking care not to damage the beads with excess heat or pressure.

Transfer both sets of stitches back onto separate ends of the 2.25mm (US 1) circular knitting needle, with the RS facing inwards and using the long tail of yarn A, work a three-needle cast off using 3.00mm (US 2/3) circular knitting needle to complete the pillow slip.

QUIVER Runner pg. 14

Debbie: for this design I took the traditional feather and fan pattern and added coloured stripes and beads to it to give it a contemporary look. There are many colour changes in the runner, so it is advisable to carry some unused yarns up the side edges to avoid multiple yarn ends. Any loose ends can be sewn into the back of the work across the knitting and into the seams where the stitches have been picked up for the edging.

Measurements

Finished size approximately: 32 x 146cm
(13 x 57½in)

Materials

Yarn
Rowan Cotton Glace: 50g (1¾oz) ball(s)

A	Ultra Marine 851 (purple)	3
B	Winsor 849 (teal)	2
C	Cadmium 846 (lime green)	2
D	Persimmon 832 (orange)	1
E	Green Slate 844 (pale teal)	2

Other
Debbie Abrahams Beads:
size 6, 500 bead pack(s)

Lipstick 207	2

Equipment
2.25mm (US 1) knitting needles
2.25mm (US 1), 80–100cm ((32–40in) circular knitting needles, two
3.00mm (US 2/3) knitting needles
Knitter's sewing or tapestry needle

Note

Some of the yarns not worked are carried up the edge of the knitting. Break off yarns when instructed.

Tension

28 sts and 46 rows to 10cm (4in) square over striped pattern using 3.00mm (US 2/3) knitting needles.

Method

Thread 420 beads onto each ball of yarn C.
Border
Using 2.25mm (US 1) knitting needles and yarn A, cast on 87 sts.
Join in yarn B.
Rows 1–2: yarn B, knit.
Rows 3–4: yarn A, knit.
Rows 5–20: repeat rows 1–4, 4 times.
Rows 21–22: yarn B, knit.
Main panel
Change to 3.00mm (US 2/3) knitting needles.
Work the following rows working repeats from Main panel only.
Join in yarn C.
Row 1 (RS): yarn C, knit.
Row 2: yarn C, purl.
Row 3: yarn C, K2, *(pb, K1, psso [this is the slipped stitch that the bead is sitting in front of]) twice, (yf, K1) 4 times, (pb, K1, psso) twice*, repeat to last st, K1.
Row 4: yarn C, knit.
Row 5: yarn A, knit.
Row 6: yarn A, purl.
Row 7: yarn A, K2, *[K2tog] twice, [yf, K1] 4 times, [K2tog] twice*; repeat from * to last st, K1.
Row 8: yarn A, knit.
Join in yarn D.
Rows 9–10: yarn D, knit.
Rows 11–18: repeat rows 1–8.
Join in yarn B.
Rows 19–20: yarn B, knit.
Rows 21–30: repeat rows 1–10.
Join in yarn E.
Row 31: yarn E, knit.
Row 32: yarn E, purl.
Row 33: yarn E, K2, *[K2tog] twice, [yf, K1] 4 times, [K2tog] twice*; repeat from * to last st, K1.
Row 34: yarn E, knit.
Rows 35–42: repeat rows 31–34 twice.
Rows 43–50: repeat rows 1–8.
Rows 51–54: repeat rows 5–8.
Rows 55–56: yarn D, knit.
Rows 57–60: yarn B, work as rows 5–8.
Rows 61–64: repeat rows 1–4.
Rows 65–76: repeat rows 5–8, 3 times.
Rows 77–78: yarn D, knit.
Rows 79–86: yarn E, work as rows 5–8, twice.

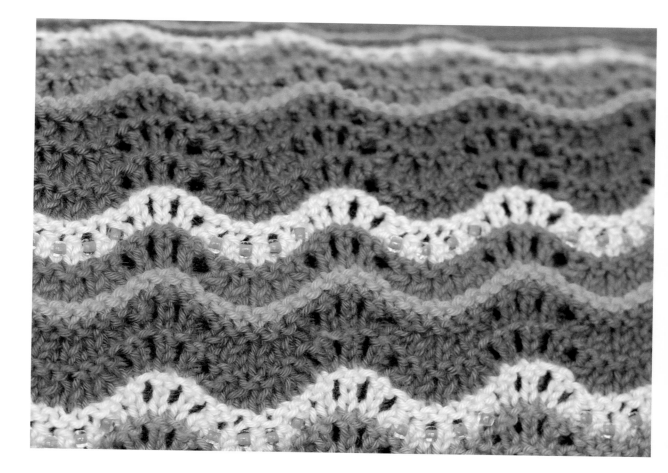

Rows 87–94: repeat rows 1–8.

Rows 95–96: yarn D, knit.

Rows 97–108: yarn B, repeat rows 31–34, 3 times.

Rows 109–112: repeat rows 1–4.

Rows 113–120: repeat rows 5–8, twice.

Rows 121–122: yarn D, knit.

Rows 123–126: yarn E, works as rows 5–8.

Rows 127–130: repeat rows 1–4.

Rows 131–142: repeat rows 5–8, 3 times.

Rows 143–144: yarn D, knit.

Rows 145–152: yarn B, work as rows 5–8, twice.

Rows 153–156: repeat rows 1–4.

Rows 157–160: repeat rows 5–8.

Rows 161–162: yarn D, knit.

Rows 163–294: repeat rows 31–162.

This is the centre of the blanket.

Starting with row 160, using the knitted fabric as a guide, work all coloured stripes, in reverse, back to the Border

Border

Change to 2.25mm (US 1) knitting needles.

Using the knitted fabric as a guide, work all coloured stripes, in reverse to cast-on.

Next row (RS): yarn A, knit.

With WS facing, using yarn A, cast off stitches knitwise.

Making up

Weave in yarn ends.

Block and press using the preferred method, taking care not to damage the beads with excess heat or pressure.

Edging

Using 2.25mm (US 1) circular knitting needles and yarn B, with RS facing, pick up and knit 447 sts along one selvedge edge of the runner.

Rows 1–2: knit.

With WS facing, cast off stitches knitwise.

Repeat these instructions for the other selvedge edge of runner.

Press the edges.

DAZZLE CUSHION pg. 50

Debbie: this is a real feast for beading fans that love to indulge in this technique. However, careful threading of the beads in the right sequence is essential to achieve the correct zig-zag pattern, so concentration levels need to be high. Having said that, the knitting itself is quite simple, a basic slip-stitch pattern combined with beading on the front panel, with two panels making up the back. So once the threading is done, you can relax and enjoy the knitting!

Measurements
Finished size approximately:
49cm (19¼in) square

Materials
Yarn
Rowan Cotton Glace: 50g (1¾oz) ball(s)

A	Ultra Marine 851 (purple)	4
B	Persimmon 832 (orange)	5

Other
Debbie Abrahams Beads:
size 6, 500 bead pack(s)

White 334	2
Orange 36	2
Black 748	2
Mauve 227	2

Buttons: 18–20mm (⅝–⅞in)

White	8

Cushion pad, 49cm (19¼in) square

Equipment
3.25mm (US 3) knitting needles
2.75mm (US 2) knitting needles
Spare 3.25mm (US 3) knitting needle
Stitch markers, two
Stitch holders or spare knitting needles, three
Knitter's sewing or tapestry needle

Tension
26 sts and 38 rows to 10cm (4in) square over slip stitch pattern using 3.25mm (US 3) knitting needles.

Note
Thread each sequence of beads onto a separate ball – three balls of yarn A and two balls of yarn B. The left over yarn from each ball can be used to knit the Upper back panel.

Method
Front panel
Thread beads onto yarn A as follows:
98 orange beads, [1 white, 5 orange] 5 times,
2 white, [5 orange, 2 white] 5 times, 5 orange, 1 white
[2 white, 5 orange, 1 white] 6 times, 3 white, [5 orange, 4 white] 5 times, 5 orange, 3 white
[2 white, 5 orange, 2 white] 6 times, [2 white, 5 orange, 2 white] 6 times,
[2 white, 4 orange, 2 white] 6 times, [2 white, 3 orange, 2 white] 6 times,
[2 white, 2 orange, 2 white] 6 times, [2 white, 1 orange, 2 white] 6 times,
60 white.
Thread beads onto yarn B following the instructions for yarn A, but using purple beads in place of orange beads and black beads in place of white beads.
Using 3.25mm (US 3) knitting needles, yarn A, cast on 135 sts.
Row 1 (chart row 1) (RS): K1, working right to left, work chart 22 st repeat patt, 6 times across each row, K2.
Row 2 (chart row 2) (WS): P2, working left to right, work chart 22 st repeat patt, 6 times across each row, P1.
Rows 3– 41: work chart rows 3–41.
Break off yarn A.
Transfer sts back to other needle so that the RS of the work is facing. Join in yarn B.
Rows 42–82: work as rows 1–41.
Break off yarn B. Join in yarn A
Rows 83–164: repeat rows 1–82, placing a stitch marker at each end of row 103 (purple band) to indicate the centre of the Front panel.
Rows 165–204: repeat rows 1-40.
Row 205 (RS): K67, K2tog, K66. (134 sts)
Leave stitches on a stitch holder or spare needle and break yarn.

Upper back panel
Using 2.75mm (US 2) knitting needles, yarn A, cast on 134 sts.
Row 1 (RS): knit.
Rows 2–5: knit.
Row 6 (WS) (buttonholes): K9, [cast off next 4 sts knitwise, K12 including the last st of cast off in count] 7 times, cast off next 4 sts knitwise, K9.
Row 7 (RS): K9, [turn work and cast on 4 sts, turn work again, K12] 7 times, turn work, cast on 4 sts, turn work again, K9.
Rows 8–13: knit.
Change to 3.25mm (US 3) knitting needles
Join in yarn B.
Row 14 (WS): yarn B, purl.

Row 15 (RS): yarn B, K3, inc in next st, K5, sl 1, K1, psso, K2tog, K5, *inc in each of next 2 sts, K5, sl 1, K1, psso, K2tog, K5; repeat from * to last 4 sts, inc in next st, K3.
Row 16: yarn B, purl.
Row 17: as row 15.
Rows 18–21: yarn A, work as rows 14-17.
Rows 22–76: repeat rows 14–21, 7 times.
Rows 77–80: repeat rows 14–17.
Leave stitches on a stitch holder or spare needle.
Break off yarn A.
Break yarn B leaving a long tail of approximately 2m (6yds).

Lower back panel
Using 3.25mm (US 3) knitting needle and yarn B, with RS facing, pick up and knit 135 sts along the cast-on edge of Front panel.
Next row (WS): purl.
Row 1 (RS): knit.
Row 2: P1, [yb, sl 1 purlwise, yf, P1] repeat to end of row.
Row 3: knit.
Row 4: P2, [yb, sl 1 purlwise, yf, P1] repeat to last st, P1.
Repeat the last 4 rows until 117 rows have been completed (or panel measures just over half the total length of the Front panel), placing a marker at each end of row 103 to indicate the halfway point.
With WS facing, cast off stitches knitwise.

Making up
Weave in yarn ends.
Block and press using the preferred method, taking care not to damage the beads with excess heat or pressure.
Transfer the stitches for Front panel and Upper back panel onto separate 3.25mm (US 3) knitting needles, with the RS facing inwards and using the long tail of yarn B, work a three-needle cast off using the spare 3.25mm (US 3) knitting needle.
Using mattress stitch, sew side seams of Lower back panel to Front panel.
Placing the upper edge of the Lower back panel under the buttonhole band of Upper back panel, stitch the Upper back panel to the Front panel – 7 chevron stripes on the Upper back panel should ease into 1 zig-zag band on the Front panel.
Attach buttons to align with buttonholes.

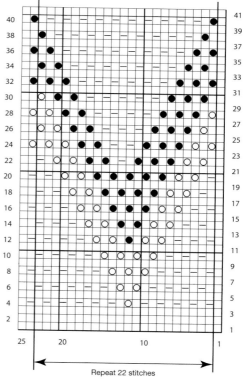

Repeat 22 stitches

☐ = K on RS, P on WS

⊟ = yb, sl 1 purlwise, yf (slip stitch, purlwise with yarn on RS of work)

Colourway one using yarn A

○ = pb (place bead), white

● = pb (place bead), orange

Colourway two using yarn D

○ = pb (place bead), black

● = pb (place bead), mauve

FURTHER INFORMATION

We have tried to make the patterns in this book as easy to follow and understand as possible, however, before starting any of the projects we do recommend that you read through the following information pages:

Seat pad – adding the backing fabric

Prepare the crochet or knit blocks as described in the Making up instructions of each pattern. Lightly press the backing fabric.

Cut from the backing fabric two pieces: one piece 44 x 44cm (17⅜ x 17⅜in) and one piece 44 x 26cm (17½ x 10¼in).

On the large fabric piece (44 x 44cm (17⅜ x 17⅜in)), along one edge (open edge) turn 3cm (1¼in) to the wrong side and press. Then turn 8cm (3¼in) to the wrong side press and stitch in place. Turn 1.5cm (⅝in) seam allowance to the wrong side along the remaining three sides.

On small fabric piece (44 x 26cm (17⅜ x 10¼in)), along one long edge (open edge) turn 2cm (⅞in) to the wrong side and press. Then turn 3cm (1⅛in) to the wrong side press and stitch in place. Turn 1.5cm (⅝in) seam allowance to the wrong side along the remaining three sides.

Place the large crochet or knit block right side facing up onto a large flat surface.

Place the large fabric piece on top with the right side facing down, the pressed edges aligned with the crochet or knit block and the open edge ending three-quarters of the way across the crochet or knit block. Pin in place, easing the fabric to the crochet or knit corners.

Place the smaller fabric piece on top with the right side facing down, the pressed edges aligned with the crochet or knit block and the open edge overlapping the open edge of the large fabric piece. Pin in place, easing the fabric to the crochet or knit corners.

Using sewing thread and backstitch sew the fabric to the crochet or knit block.

Turn the right side out.

Felting

The correct name for this process is fulling. Using a mild detergent, wash the pieces in a washing machine on a gentle wool-wash. DO NOT tumble-dry. Gently stretch the fabric into shape and leave to dry. Repeat the washing process until the felted fabric has the desired appearance.

Crochet Terminology:

UK and US crochet terminology is not the same. All patterns within this book are written using UK terminology. Below is a list of the US equivalents:

UK	US
double crochet – dc	single crochet - sc
half treble crochet - htr	half double crochet – hdc
treble crochet – tr	double crochet – dc
double treble crochet – dtr	treble crochet – tr
triple treble crochet – trtr	double treble crochet – dtr

Abbreviations – Crochet

Here is a list of common crochet abbreviations. Abbreviations can alter depending on whether you are following a UK or US written pattern and can also be personal to a certain pattern writer or designer. It is important that you always check you have the correct understanding of an abbreviation. For a full list of UK & US terminology see above.

alt	alternate
approx.	approximately
beg	beginning
ch(s)	chain(s)
ch sp	chain space
cl	cluster
cm	centimeter
cont	continue
dec	decrease
foll	following
gr	group
inc	increase
nxt	next
rem	remaining
rep	repeat

RS	right side
sl	slip
ss	slip stitch
st(s)	stitch(es)
tch	turning chain
tog	together
yo	yarn over
WS	wrong side

Abbreviations - Knit

cont	continue
c3b	slip next 2 stitches onto cable needle and hold at back of work, knit next stitch from left-hand needle, then knit stitches from cable needle
foll/s	following/follows
inc	increase one stitch by working into the front and then the back of the stitch
K	knit
K2tog	knit two stitches together
LH	left-hand
P	purl
patt	pattern
pb	place bead (on right-side and wrong-side rows): with yarn on the right-side of the work, slide a bead up the yarn, slip the next stitch purlwise, then if necessary bring the yarn between the needles to work the next stitch, leaving the bead at the front of the work
psso	pass slipped stitch over
P3tog	purl three stitches together
rem	remaining
RS	right-side
sl	slip
st/sts	stitch/stitches
WS	wrong–side
yb	take yarn back between needles(away from you)
yf (or yo)	bring yarn forward between needles (towards you)
yrn (or yo)	yarn round needle

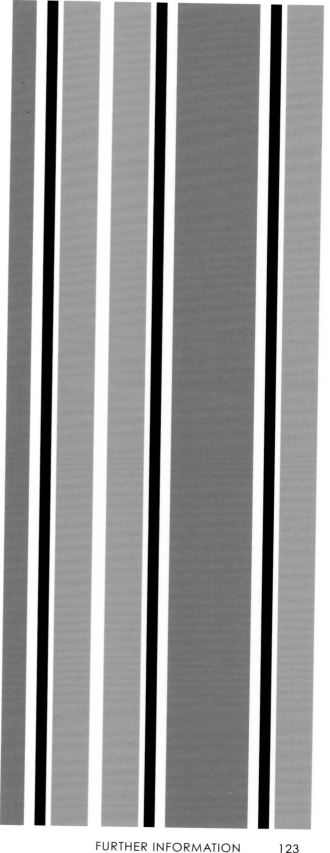

TECHNICAL STUFF

Kaleidoscope is aimed at knitters and crocheters who have a good knowledge of their crafts. However, as a gentle reminder we have listed here some of the key techniques used in the book.

There are many good books on the market that act as great learning tools for both knitting and crochet. We recommend 'The Ultimate Knitting Bible' by Sharon Brant and 'The Ultimate Crochet Bible' by Jane Crowfoot as good reference books.

The Internet can also be of a massive help when looking for support with your techniques. We recommend you make Youtube your first port of call when searching for guidance, as video tutorials are usually the perfect way to learn.

To help specifically with all those important finishing techniques and to learn some great tips and professional techniques, you can purchase Debbie Abrahams' DVD, which is available via her web site: www.debbieabrahams.com/site/shop/dvds

Below you will find a list of techniques included within this book which you may want help with:

Knit Techniques:

Bobble: increase the number of knitted stitches by knitting into the front and then the back of a single stitch until you have the required number. Work on these stitches only until the bobble is the required size. Right Side facing, work stitches together so that one stitch remains

Intarsia: intarsia is used when you want to work a motif design over a relatively large number of stitches, create a single thickness of knitted fabric, when a colour is not repeatedly used and when you wish to have no floats at the reverse of the work.

Yarns are wound onto separate bobbins and used independently. At the point where the shade changes, you need to cross the yarn you have finished using over the yarn you are about to use to avoid getting a hole in your work.

Kitchener Stitch: this stitch creates an invisible seam and is worked using a knitters sewing needle and a length of yarn on live stitches; therefore stitches are not cast off once the knitted fabric is completed, instead a row of knitting is replicated by sewing through the live stitches.

Placing beads on the right side of the work: bring a bead up to the top of the yarn so that it sits as close as possible to the knitting needle. Yarn forward between needles, slip the next stitch purlwise, take the yarn back between needles holding bead in place in front of the slipped stitch, knit next stitch and continue in pattern as set.

Placing beads on the wrong side of the work: bring a bead up to the top of the yarn so that it sits as close as possible to the knitting needle. Yarn back between needles, slip the next stitch purlwise, bring yarn forward between needles holding bead in place in front of the slipped stitch, purl next stitch and continue in pattern as set.

Wrap stitches: a wrap stitch avoids a gap between stitches when working and turning. To wrap a stitch, move the yarn to the opposite side of the work between the needles, slip the next stitch purl wise and then move the yarn back to its' original position, turn and continue in pattern as set.
Once all the wraps are complete you will need to knit or purl across the row, moving the wrap stitches to the reverse of the work as you do so. This neatens the work and removes potential holes.

Removing a wrap on the right side of the work: slide your right-hand needle underneath the wrap and knit it together with the next stitch on the left-hand needle.

Removing a wrap on the wrong side of the work: slide your right-hand needle underneath the wrap from the front side of the work, lift it onto the left-hand needle and purl it together with the next stitch.

Three-needle cast off: do not cast off once the knitted fabric is complete. Place two knitted pieces (with the same stitch count) on spare needles with the right side of both pieces facing inwards. Cast off the stitches, knitting one stitch from each needle simultaneously so that both stitches are cast off at the same time.

Crochet Techniques:

Bobble: using a stitch with a long post, such as a treble or double treble crochet (US double or treble crochet) for example, increase the number of stitches by working into a single stitch until you have the required number, stopping one step before the end of the stitch for each stitch made so that you have an accumulation of loops on the crochet hook. Yarn round hook, draw through all loops on the hook to complete.

Beaded double crochet: with wrong side facing, bring a bead up to the top of the yarn so that it sits as close as possible to the crochet hook. Work a double crochet stitch (US single crochet) catching the yarn beyond the bead on the first step of the stitch. Complete the stitch as usual and continue in pattern as set.

Beaded treble crochet: with wrong side facing, complete a treble crochet stitch (US double crochet) as usual stopping after the first part of the stitch post is made and 2 loops of yarn remain on the hook. Bring a bead up to the top of the yarn so that it sits as close as possible to the crochet hook. Complete the stitch, catching the yarn beyond the bead on the next step of the stitch. Complete the stitch as usual and continue in pattern as set.

Changing yarn on the final step of the stitch: when joining in a new yarn shade it is advisable to do so before you complete the last step of the stitch before the change is required. For example, when working a treble crochet, work until 2 loops of yarn remain on the hook and the last stage of the stitch remains incomplete. Hold the new yarn at the reverse of the work, yarn over hook and draw through to complete the stitch. The loop on the hook will be in the new shade

Jacquard: as for 'fairisle' knitted equivalent. A technique where a double thickness of fabric is produced to create repeated colour patterns. The yarn is carried across the reverse side of the work when not in use. When carrying for more than 3 stitches you will need to weave in the yarn on the reverse side of the work and it is important that you achieve an even tension to avoid puckering.

Intarsia: as for 'Intarsia' knitted equivalent, but changing yarn shade on the final step of the stitch before the colour change

Surface crochet: this creates the appearance of a sewn chain stitch on the right side of the fabric.

Stockists:

Rowan Yarns
Green Lane Mill
Holmfirth
West Yorkshire
HD9 2DX
www.knitrowan.com

Debbie Abrahams Beads
26 Church Drive
Nottingham
NG5 2BA
www.debbieabrahamsbeads.co.uk

Duttons For Buttons
Oxford Street
Harrogate
North Yorkshire
HG1 1QE
www.duttonsforbuttons.co.uk

Bag Clasps
5 Dorchester Close
Thornton-Cleveleys
Lancashire
FY5 5BZ
www.bag-clasps.co.uk

DESIGNER PROFILES

DEBBIE ABRAHAMS

Debbie Abrahams has been passionate about hand-knitting ever since she first picked up a pair of knitting needles at the tender age of six. With both her parents and two sisters being artistically trained, it was inevitable that Debbie would pursue a career in design.

Firmly focussed on hand-knitting, she applied directly from school to Nottingham Trent University to do a BA (Hons) degree in Knitwear Design. Soon after graduating, her association with Rowan began and she has worked for them as a freelance consultant for the past seventeen years whilst gradually establishing her own hand-knitting business.

Debbie chose to focus on designing accessories, and for her this is the perfect vehicle to explore what she loves most about the craft: "For me, knitting has endless possibilities, especially when you start combining colour with stitch structure and embellishment. Knitting with beads is something that I really love and with my husband running the Debbie Abrahams Beads business, it is tempting for me to put a bit of sparkle into everything that I knit!" Debbie's inspiration comes mainly from graphical sources and she has a vast collection of visuals to motivate her including greeting cards, ceramics and fabrics.

She is the author of five books, with Kaleidoscope being her sixth title. She supports her books and collections through an intensive programme of workshops, visiting knitting shops and groups across the UK and America. Keen to share her expertise with fellow knitters, this is something that Debbie thrives on and believes is one of the main reasons behind her success: "To meet the people who are buying my books and knitting up my designs is so important to me. And workshops give me this opportunity. Without their continued support I would not be enjoying the success that I am."

In more recent years, Debbie's Mystery Blanket Club has become a major part of her business and it has captured the imagination of knitters all over the world. She designs a unique blanket every year and knitters sign up to join the club for ten months. The theme is kept a secret throughout and is only revealed as the blanket starts to take shape. Debbie has expanded this idea to include an annual Mystery Cushion Club with a project designed exclusively for members only.

Debbie has a website through which you can find out all about her Clubs, workshops and kits: www.debbieabrahams.com

You can contact her by email at: info@debbieabrahams.com

JANE CROWFOOT

Jane Crowfoot has always had a love for yarn and all things crafty, and attributes her 'crochet gene' to her Great Grandmother, Alice, who was seldom seen without a crochet hook in her hand and a few granny squares upon her lap.

Jane was taught to knit as a child and after showing a flair for art throughout school she decided to do a foundation course in art and design before going on to do a degree in textile design at Winchester School of Art, specializing in constructed textiles. Jane has worked as a freelance designer and design consultant for the past 15 years and has worked closely with both Debbie Bliss and Rowan Yarns.

Although an accomplished knitter, Jane has a passion for crochet, which is currently seeing a huge upsurge in popularity across the world. "I think it is far more organic and requires less planning when designing. I often start a project without any clear idea of what the finished product will be. Crochet pieces can start small, perhaps with just a flower motif which will fit the palm of your hand, yet they can end up being large enough to act as a cushion cover or a throw."Jane gets much of her inspiration from interior magazines, and she loves looking at greetings cards and wrapping paper.

Despite working as a designer for many years, Jane thinks it's only recently that she has begun to find her own style of work. "It's only now that my kids have grown up a bit that I have more of my own time to develop." Jane loves playing with colour and says she is constantly drawn to artists such as Raoul Dufy and Paul Chagal for inspiration on colour combinations. Jane has a love of exotic textiles such as Indian saris and Japanese screens, although it is retro patterns of the 50s, 60s and 70s that currently have her inspired.

Following in Debbie Abrahams' footsteps and on her recom-mendation, Jane runs a successful crochet club, which provides participants with the chance to complete an exclusive throw/blanket project over the course of 6 months. Jane's design theme for the project is not a complete mystery as she releases teaser images in advance of the start of the project. Members live across the globe and Jane provides an on-line dedicated blog which includes tips & techniques and step-by-step images to aid crocheters along the way.

Jane is the author of 5 titles of which Kaleidoscope is the most recent. Past titles are: Finishing Techniques for Handknitters, Two Stitch Knits, The Ultimate Crochet Bible and Homespun Vintage. Jane has her own company, 'Janie Crow Ltd'. Check out the website to find more designs and a range of accessories.

You can also 'like' the company page on Facebook and Ravelry and also follow Jane on Twitter @JaneCrowfoot

www.janiecrow.co.uk

ACKNOWLEDGEMENTS

We have been lucky that so many people have lent their support to us while we followed our dream and set about creating Kaleidoscope. A project like this takes a huge amount of work and there are many people who deserve a vote of thanks…..

Designing the projects in this book came really easily to both of us – each and every one was a pleasure as we were so enthused by the concept of the book and by our design inspiration. However our ideas would not have made it to fruition without our invaluable team of knitters, crocheters and stitchers. For their wonderful skills, big love to Annette Traves, Amanda Golland, Donna Grossman, Eleanor Yates, Erica Pask, Hannah Kennedy, Heddy Abrahams, Heather Esswood, Jenny Still, Liz Jenks, Mary Leeson, Nicola Hale and Sharon Tyler.

We would like to thank Michael Wicks for all his lovely photographs, Tanya & Philip Taylor, the owners of the fabulous 'Tea House', for being so welcoming and helpful on shoot day, and Julie & Steve in Nottingham, who gave us access to their lovely home.

We are so grateful to our invaluable copy editor, pattern checker, lunch provider and delicious cake maker Luise Roberts and our editor Juliet Bernard for giving us support and advice throughout. And a big thank you to Rowan Yarns for providing us with all that lovely yarn to play with!

Whopping thanks go to designer Darren Brant who managed to turn our idea into a tangible thing and was on hand to guide and help us at every turn.

Finally we would like to thank Andy and Steve for being our constant and loyal companions and sounding boards - you both deserve a medal! Debbie will knit you both one and Jane will add a nice crochet border!

A Dedication:

For Sue, Culli, Bix & Bebop